THE SOCIAL CONSTRUCTION OF SEXUAL HARASSMENT LAW

The Social Construction of Sexual Harassment Law

The role of the national, organizational and individual context

MIA L. CAHILL
Visiting Scholar, Institute for Law and Society
New York University

Routledge
Taylor & Francis Group
LONDON AND NEW YORK

First published 2001 by Dartmouth Publishing Company and Ashgate Publishing

Reissued 2018 by Routledge
2 Park Square, Milton Park, Abingdon, Oxon OX14 4RN
711 Third Avenue, New York, NY 10017, USA

Routledge is an imprint of the Taylor & Francis Group, an informa business

A Library of Congress record exists under LC control number: 00135338

ISBN 13: 978-1-138-63648-4 (hbk)
ISBN 13: 978-1-138-63649-1 (pbk)
ISBN 13: 978-1-315-20381-2 (ebk)

Contents

Acknowledgments

I owe many thanks to those who have guided me through the intellectual beginnings and final stages of this project. I would like to thank Lauren Edelman, Howard Erlanger, Marc Galanter, Charles Halaby and Mark Suchman of the University of Wisconsin for their generosity with their time and words as I was implementing this study and beyond. I also wish to thank many at the Institute for Law and Society at New York University. I am grateful to Wolf Heydebrand, Christine Harrington, Jo Dixon, Eric Feldman and others at the Institute for Law and Society for their comments as I developed this study into the present book.

I also wish to thank my many mentors and friends who helped me shape these ideas before, during and after completion of this study. Valerie Hans, Joyce Sterling and Nancy Reichman provided invaluable comments on my work. Further, Katarina Zippel and Abigail Saguy, who shared my interest in international sexual harassment law, helped shape this book.

I received funding from several sources that enabled me to complete this project. The Hewlett Foundation supported the earliest stages of this research by funding me as a Hewlett Fellow at the Institute for Legal Studies at the University of Wisconsin. After the initial stages were complete, I received a National Science Foundation Dissertation Grant that made the cross-national research possible. I received a University of Wisconsin fellowship when I returned to the United States to support my dissertation writing. The Department of Sociology of the University of Wisconsin also provided a travel grant and a small grant to facilitate my work on this project. Finally, the support of the Institute for Law and Society at New York University enabled the completion of this project.

I also wish to thank the participants in Austria and in the United States who gave their time and thoughtfulness to make this study possible.

Finally, I am indebted to my family for their support in this process. My husband Matthew Sanidas, my children Madison Cahill-Sanidas and Alexander Cahill-Sanidas, as well as my parents and in-laws Teena Cahill, Brooks Dyer, James Cahill, Ellen Cahill, Frieda Sanidas and John Sanidas, all provided support and encouragement for the completion of this project.

1 Introduction

Law and its Social Context

Scholars have long considered the relationship between law and its social context. However, too often, operationalizations of social context are limited to a single level, such as national context (for example, Trubek and Galanter, 1974), organizational context (for example, Blumberg, 1967) or individual context (for example, Ewick and Silbey, 1998). While perceptions of law do vary across cultures, within organizations or among individuals, until now, no one has considered the significance of variation at all three levels. This study expands our notion of social context and shows how it fundamentally influences the understandings and implementation of legal rules. It explores empirically perceptions of law at three levels of social context: the national context, the organizational or corporate context and the individual, or sociodemographic, context. Each level of social context comes with the potential to introduce variability into the social understanding of what law is, and to interact with the other two levels.

In no area of law is social context more important than in sexual harassment law. While relatively new to the legal arena, today, sexual harassment law is a firmly established legal wrong in the United States and Austria, as well as in many other countries around the globe. The mere mention of the term 'sexual harassment' engenders reactions that range from righteous condemnation of sexualizing women in the workplace to cries of 'political correctness' gone awry. The range of reactions to sexual harassment is the result of differing perceptions of both the social problem of sexual harassment and its solutions in law. Like other legal issues that have transcended the domain of professional discourse, the social significance of sexual harassment goes far beyond its use as fodder for late-night television hosts.

Feminists fought to protect the rights of women at work by advocating that sexual harassment be seen as a social problem with a legal solution in sex discrimination law. They were supported by the United States Equal Employment Opportunity Commission (EEOC) in 1980, when they issued guidelines on sex discrimination that included sexual harassment. Sexual harassment, as a type of sex discrimination, was recognized by the US Supreme Court six years later (*Meritor Savings Bank* v. *Vinson*, 477 U.S. 54 (1986)).[1]

The topic of sexual harassment was slowly gaining status as a social problem and a legal issue in the USA when interest in the issue exploded during the 1991 Senate confirmation hearings of Clarence Thomas. Law professor Anita Hill was called to testify before the Senate Judiciary Committee about her statements alleging Justice Thomas's sexual harassment. The Senate ultimately confirmed the appointment of Thomas to serve on the US Supreme Court with a Senate vote of 52 to 48. At the time, public opinion polls reflected popular support for Justice Thomas's denial of sexual harassment (Sanger, 1992).

The issue of sexual harassment remained an issue of national and international debate after the hearings, raising consciousness of the issue, if not necessarily sympathy for it. In 1997, the Supreme Court allowed a sexual harassment civil suit brought by former Arkansas state employee Paula Jones against President Clinton to proceed while he is in office. Although the case was later dismissed, the president's testimony in that case was the legal justification for his ensuing impeachment trial in the US Senate, which received extensive press coverage abroad. More than any other aspect of sex discrimination law, sexual harassment has been the object of considerable public debate and interest.

Sexual harassment law is an especially interesting law to examine because of the worldwide dominance of early US legal conceptualizations of sexual harassment, making it amenable to comparisons of similar law within different social context. The roots of an 'international convergence of sexual harassment law' (Earle and Madek, 1993:43) are often attributed to the USA, with comparative studies proclaiming sexual harassment 'made in America, by women' (Bernstein, 1994: 1227; Webb, 1994).[2] While certainly an over-simplification, the dominance of the US legal model of sexual harassment, as codified in the 1980 EEOC Guidelines, is undeniable. Although European countries vary in the degree to which they relied on the US legal conception of sexual harassment, with some countries, such as France, adopting law as a *foil* to the US model, it is this legal model, and the US cultural association with sexual harassment, with which all other national regulations must contend. It was the year after the Justice Thomas confirmation that Austria adopted a sexual harassment law.

In Austria, the push for sexual harassment legislation came later than in the USA, but when a sexual harassment law was finally adopted, it was striking in its similarity to the EEOC Guidelines. The laws of sexual harassment in the USA and Austria were chosen as the sites of this study because of the striking similarity in the substance of the sexual harassment laws in these two countries. Both Austrian and US law place sexual harassment within the context of sex discrimination law, and define the legal *harm* of sexual harassment very similarly.[3] While the legal definition of the harm of sexual harassment in the USA and Austria is substantially similar, the laws exist in very different legal systems and very different national contexts (Cahill, The Illusion of Precedent, 1996; 1999).[4] This selection made it possible to isolate the role of national context on understandings of law.

In this study, I focus on three components of the *national context*. First, there is the formal law and legal system including statutes, court decisions, legal rules and regulatory guidelines. While the legal definition of sexual harassment is similar in the USA and Austria, there are substantial differences in the structure of the legal systems. Second, the national context includes legal culture or the norms associated with law, such as the emergence of sexual harassment law, the acceptance of legal claims for immaterial damages, access to lawyers and judicial receptivity to claims. Finally, the third component of national context is social norms.

To examine the role of the organizational context, I conducted five case studies of organizations similar in size, industry and gender composition of employees, but existing in different national sites: either the USA or Austria. I empirically focus on two aspects of the organizational context in the study: organizational characteristics, such as industry, size and employee composition, and organizational culture, including the beliefs, patterns and practices internal to the firm. I rely on these five organizational case studies to explore the influence of organizational context – as part of the social context – on the understandings and implementation of sexual harassment law.

Finally, I consider the role of individual differences, adding the third layer to my conceptualization of social context. To explore the variation among individuals in their perceptions of sexual harassment law, I focus on sociodemographic categories, such as sex and age, as well as differences in attitudes about law in general, or sex discrimination law in particular. *These three layers together, the national context, the organizational context and the individual context, provide the social context through which law is understood.*

It seems almost simplistic to claim that social context influences perceptions and understandings of law, but, indeed, this is a claim that challenges the dominant discourse of law by policy makers and many scholars. In this, the prevailing legal centrist view, law is knowable, hierarchically handed down from the state and codified in formal laws. Even many social science scholars describe law as a one-dimensional construct, relying heavily on the legal centrist vision of law (for example, Powell and DiMaggio, 1991; Fligstein, 1985; Sutton *et al.*, 1994; Guthrie and Roth, 1999). Comparative legal theorists too, tend to rely on too literal definitions of the formal law to explain differences in both law and practice, overlooking variation in perceptions of law (for example, Lester, 1995; Lipper, 1992; Bernstein, 1994; 1996; Weiss, 1993; Fredrickson, 1995).

Law and society scholars have long countered this singular vision of law. They contend that the legal centrist view overlooks the ambiguity (Edelman, 1992; Suchman and Edelman, 1996) and the contested nature of law and legal authority (Ewick and Silbey, 1998). In the law and society perspective, law itself is a cultural construct, reflecting the power relations, priorities, symbols and ideologies of society at a particular point in time. In other words, 'law' is understood through its social context.

While legal understandings are a product of social context, they also constitute categories that limit and define social action, framing the very nature of social action, legal mobilization and enforcement (Tushnet, 1984; McCann, 1992; Ewick and Silbey, 1998). The formal law provides the boundaries and constitutive categories of legal understandings. Rather than merely responding to law, 'corporations', as legal categories, are defined by it. But there is a leap from the formal law, what the law is, to what actually happens in practice that is generally overlooked by many scholars and policy makers. Law is defined, not just by what it states or purports to do, but by *how it is understood* by those who might use it, or defend against it.

This two-sided understanding of law makes its analyses even more complex. While certainly there exists 'law', just what the law is, and what it means, is much more difficult to observe, much less know. This vision of law, as a continuing cultural process, implies that the demands of law are rarely clear-cut and unambiguous, a characteristic of sexual harassment law (Erlanger *et al.*, 1987; Abzug and Mezias, 1993; Suchman and Cahill, 1996). As McCann describes it, law is 'a complex repertoire of discursive strategies and symbolic frameworks that structure ongoing social intercourse and meaning-making activity among citizens... legal conventions... [that] are inherently indeterminate, pluralistic and contingent in actual social practice' (McCann, 1992: 282). To engage in a cultural study of law so conceptualized, Kahn (1999: 91) suggests that we stand apart from 'normative inquiries' about law and 'move scholarship... toward this description of the world of meaning that is the rule of law'. To do this, I focus on the three levels of social context that provide the means of legal understanding: national context, organizational context and individual context. Given this multifaceted view of law, it is almost unimaginable to examine law *without* a role for culture, or social context.

The Study Design

To explore the role social context plays on legal understandings and implementation, I selected five organizational case studies. By using the similarity of law as my basis, I ask how the national context, the organizational context and individual context, contribute to variation in perceptions of law.

Table 1.1 identifies the five case studies. They relate to two firms in the USA, one firm in Austria and two firms that cross boundaries: US multinationals operating in Austria. Controlling for as many differences as possible, the chosen firms were matched according to industry (pharmaceutical[5]), organizational size (the mean and median number of employees is 56) and employee composition (42–60 per cent female employees).

These organizational characteristics were chosen as controls because of their potential relationship to understandings of law. The firms share another similarity: none of them had ever had a sexual harassment lawsuit at the organizational site, although they were not intentionally selected on this characteristic. The firms are known in this study under their pseudonyms to protect confidentiality. They are Gulf Stream, Jet Stream (the US multinationals), Hudson and Prairie (the US domestic firms), and Alpen, the Austrian firm.

Table 1.1 Selection of organizations

Organization	USA	Austria
Domestic	Hudson Prairie	Alpen
US multinational		Jet Stream Gulf Stream

I used a two-pronged approach to explore understandings of sexual harassment law at these firms. First, I gathered documents and information from the managers at each of the firms relating to the understanding and implementation of sexual harassment law within the organization. Second, I distributed questionnaires to employees at each of the organizations relating to understandings of sexual harassment law and support for its implementation within the organization.

Interviews began in Austria in November 1995, just after Austria had agreed to join the European Union in full, and ended in May 1997. Because the firms are relatively small, the CEO was personally involved in any existing sexual harassment policymaking at the firm. I interviewed the CEO,[6] and any other manager who would be involved in issues concerning sexual harassment policy or disputes at each of the firms.[7] All of the managers participating in the study were male, well-educated and spoke English.[8] The use of semi-structured interviews meant that data acquired included not just the formal organizational responses to law, characteristic of research in this area, but also the ways in which managers conceptualize and understand the requirements of law. The interviews centered around managers' definitions of sexual harassment, formal and informal procedures for dispute resolution, litigation, management and employee training on sexual harassment, organizational culture and the informal and formal responses to sexual harassment law.

To gather information about employee understandings of law, I distributed a survey at four of the five firms.[9] The survey was either in English or German, depending on the site (Austrian sites received the German-version survey). The overall response rate was 57 per cent, which is high for organizational surveys. The main body of the survey consists of vignettes, where the employee was asked to determine whether or not the conduct described is legally considered sexual harassment and how the organization should best address the incident. The responses reflect the employees' understandings of sexual harassment law and its implementation.

I explore employee understandings of law by examining individual responses to three sexual harassment vignettes, which fall into the three categories of sexual harassment established by researchers: gender harassment, seductive behavior and sexual imposition (Gefland *et al.*, 1995; Fitzgerald and Hesson-McInnis, 1989). Of the three vignettes, 'sexual imposition' most clearly falls under the legal harm defined by sexual harassment law. 'Seductive Behavior', also sexual in nature, is less severe. The 'Gender Harassment' example defines harassing behavior that is gendered, but not sexual in nature, a type of sexual harassment unlikely to be supported in US or Austrian courts (see Chapter 3). It is the goal of this project to examine, not what particular aspects of the vignettes would cause employees to find behavior more or less sexually harassing, but what shapes these understandings. On the basis of these data, and of information about the organization provided by the managers, I explore whether Austrian and US employees differ on the limits they attribute to law, and their support for the organization in implementing sexual harassment law. Further details on the methods of this study may be found in Appendix I.

In the next chapter, I describe the empirical study and the various aspects of social context this book explores. I begin with the national level of social context in Chapter 2. There, I trace the emergence of sexual harassment law in the USA and Austria. I further detail the law of sexual harassment in the two countries in Chapter 3, including the striking similarity in the ways the harm of sexual harassment are legally defined. Chapter 4 marks the presentation of the organizational case studies. In this chapter, I describe the perceptions of law by managers within these firms and show the distinct roles of both national and organizational context as components of social context. In

Chapters 5 and 6, I present the quantitative analyses of individual perceptions of law by focusing on the employees at each of these firms. There, I find variation in legal understandings and support for its implementation based on national, organizational and individual aspects of the social context. Finally, I present my conclusions and discuss the implications of my findings in Chapter 7.

Notes

1 As further detailed in Chapter 3, sexual harassment is defined as 'Unwelcome sexual advances, requests for sexual favors, and other verbal or physical conduct of a sexual nature' (*Vinson*, at 66). There are two legal categories of sexual harassment: quid pro quo and hostile environment (ibid., 65–7). Quid pro quo harassment occurs when submission to the unwelcome sexual conduct is 'made either explicitly or implicitly a term or condition of an individual's employment... or used as the basis for employment decisions affecting such individual' (Equal Employment Opportunity Commission, 1991, 'Guidelines on Discrimination Because of Sex', 29, C.F.R. 1604.11(a)). Hostile environment sexual harassment occurs when the unwelcome sexual conduct 'has the purpose or effect of unreasonably interfering with an individual's work performance or creating an intimidating, hostile, or offensive working environment' (ibid.).

2 Depending on how fine-toothed one's comb is, there are probably as many differences as similarities in international treatments of sexual harassment (for example, Saguy, 1998; Bernstein, 1997; Elman, 1996; Webb, 1994; Lester, 1995; DeJean, 1993; Husbands, 1992; Lipper, 1992).

3 The sexual harassment law in Austria, as incorporated within the Equal Treatment Act (*Gleichbehandlungsgesetz*) is almost identical to the EEOC Guidelines on Sexual Harassment (1991) in the USA.

4 In the USA, the dominant language is English; in Austria, it is German. Geographically, Austria is located in Europe between the former Eastern Bloc countries and Western Europe, while the USA is on the North American continent. Austria has a population of approximately five million, with high homogeneity of race and religion (Catholicism), while the USA has a population of 270 million with less homogeneity of race and religion.

5 The pharmaceutical industry was chosen because of its international character, the large number of firms in Austria, and because of the high potential for access through personal contacts.

6 CEO, described as the head of the organizational site, was sometimes called an executive manager by the firms.

7 At the time of the interviews, just one firm (the US domestic firm, Prairie) had a personnel manager whose responsibilities included potentially resolving sexual harassment claims. Other firms were in the process of creating this position, or the position was currently vacant. In addition, none of these organizations had an in-house counsel whose role included the resolution of sexual harassment disputes. Other managers were interviewed if they would potentially be involved in issues regarding sexual harassment.

8 At Hudson, I also interviewed the female administrative assistant to the CEO because of her role as a sexual harassment liaison officer. I interviewed a total of ten managers.

9 I distributed surveys to all employees through their mailboxes and they were returned by mail directly to me. The fifth firm did not participate in the survey component of this study.

2 The Social Context of Sexual Harassment: the National Level

The Emergence of Sexual Harassment as a Legal Wrong in the United States

Sexual harassment was not originally conceived in the passage of the 1964 Civil Rights Act when Congress included protections for sex discrimination along with the hard-fought racial discrimination protections of the civil rights movement. In the passing of the Act, the word 'sex' was added late in congressional debate by Congressman Howard Smith. Sex discrimination protections were likely an ill-fated attempt to kill the bill benefitting minorities. However, discrimination protections for women were not completely without support inside and outside Congress. Congressman Smith had been supportive of (white) women's rights in the past, and the ban on sex discrimination was supported in earnest by a coalition of five congresswomen and women's rights groups outside Congress (Saguy, 1999; Bird, 1997). As passed, Title VII of the Act states:

> It shall be an unlawful employment practice for an employer (1) to fail or refuse to hire or to discharge any individual, or otherwise to discriminate against any individual with respect to his compensation, terms, conditions, or privileges of employment because of such individual's race, color, religion, *sex*, or national origin. (Civil Rights Act of 1964, 42 U.S.C. Sec. 2000e-2 (1988), emphasis added)[1]

Nevertheless, because the statute itself makes no mention of *sexual harassment*, the wording prohibiting sex discrimination has been the sole basis for sexual harassment claims under the Act. Through the combined influence of feminist groups, lawsuits, media attention and government action, sexual harassment was clearly defined as a social problem with a legal solution within the Civil Rights Act by the mid-1980s.

The first legal challenges of sexual harassment appeared in the mid-1970s, right at the peak of the modern feminist movement in the USA. Prominent groups of the movement, such as the National Organization for Women and the National Women's Political Caucus, supported the work of two activist groups opposed to sexual harassment and worked to increase its recognition as a social problem. The first, Working Women United, and its research branch Working Women's Institute, was organized in 1975 to protest against sexual harassment and, later, to counsel victims (Weeks *et al.*, 1986). The following year, the Alliance Against Sexual Coercion (AASC) similarly worked to raise media awareness and to aid sexual harassment victims (Weeks *et al.*, 1986; Elman, 1996a).

With the issue of sexual harassment gaining in media prominence, victims began turning to the courts (and initially losing) in the mid-1970s. In *Barnes* v. *Train*,[2] for example, an Environmental Protection Agency clerk claimed that her job was eliminated because she refused to have sexual relations with her supervisor, a claim we know today as quid pro quo sexual harassment. Reasoning that she was fired because of her refusal to have sexual relations rather than because of discrimination based on sex, as Title VII of the 1964 Civil Rights Act requires, the trial judge ruled against her claim. Similar claims were made and initially lost at the trial level (for example, *Tomkins* v. *Public Service Electric and Gas Co.*).[3] However, by the end of the 1970s, appeals courts began to recognize a legal claim of sexual harassment. In a 1977 appeal of the *Barnes* case, the Appeals Court found that the plaintiff was indeed a victim of sex discrimination in employment, and ruled in her favor.[4] The Courts of Appeals in the fourth and third circuits made similar rulings, finding that sexual harassment was covered under Title VII of the Civil Rights Act of 1964 as a type of sex discrimination, and were soon followed by other circuits on appeal.[5] These early cases marked the beginning of definitions relying on the conceptualization of sexual harassment as a *discrimination*.

In the late 1970s, two books added to the legitimacy and publicity of sexual harassment. They foreshadowed waves of sexual harassment research and cases to come. In *Sexual Shakedown*, Lin Farley (1978) describes incidents of sexual harassment and, even though she was a journalist, brought the issue of sexual harassment to the attention of researchers. The following year, the first congressional hearing on sexual harassment began before the House's Committee on Post Office and Civil Service, where plans to conduct a systematic study of the sexual harassment of federal workers were developed (see Weeks *et al.*, 1986). The ensuing survey by the US Merit Systems Protection Board Survey (1981, 1988) of approximately 20 000 male and female federal workers provided the basis for much of the early scholarly research on sexual harassment.

The first widely publicized study of sexual harassment was based on the responses of *Harvard Business Review* and *Redbook Magazine* subscribers. In a media sensation, this study found that 90 per cent of the female respondents had been sexually harassed, and declared sexual harassment a pervasive problem in the workplace (Collins and Blodgett, 1981). However, there were serious methodological concerns in generalizing the survey results. The study reported the responses of those magazine subscribers who bothered returning the survey – surely raising the specter of response bias.[6] Nevertheless, this study marked the peak of newspaper, magazine and journal coverage of sexual harassment to date (Weeks *et al.*, 1986).[7] With media attention focused on the issue of sexual harassment, activists lobbied state governments to extend legal protection to sexual harassment victims who left or were dismissed from their workplaces.

As the case for sexual harassment was made in the media, Congress and state legislatures, plaintiffs began to challenge the courts in earnest with sexual harassment cases. In doing so, they relied on a legal argument set out by Catherine MacKinnon in *Sexual Harassment of Working Women*. While her book was published in 1978, early drafts of the legal argument circulated in the legal community and this draft was even used by a law clerk in the *Barnes* v. *Costle* decision (Saguy, 1999; Weeks *et al.*, 1986).

MacKinnon's legal argument, which would eventually become the dominant definition of sexual harassment, went like this: sexual harassment in employment contributed to the sexual coercion of women by men, and was therefore sex-based discrimination as understood within Title VII of the 1964 Civil Rights Act. Central to MacKinnon's legal argument is that sexual harassment is *group-based* harm, falling under the discrimination statute, rather than *individual harm*, which would fall under state tort law. As this was a type of discrimination based on sex, women as a group should receive the protections of civil rights law. As Saguy (1999) observes, this discrimination frame had lasting effects on the development of sexual harassment in the USA. In 1980, at the turn of the decade, 75 sexual harassment lawsuits were filed (Feary, 1994).

MacKinnon's (1978) path-breaking argument distinguished two types of sexual harassment: *quid pro quo* and *hostile environment* harassment. These categories were soon used by the Equal Employment Opportunity Commission, the US Supreme Court and, over a decade later, by parliaments around the world. In 1980, the EEOC, the government agency charged with enforcing Title VII, issued regulatory guidelines defining sexual harassment as a type of sex discrimination under Title VII of the Civil Rights Act. EEOC guidelines do not have the force of law, but are meant as the Commission's interpretation of the Civil Rights Act. It is up to the federal courts to determine their impact on any particular case.[8] However, the promulgation of the guidelines would prove to be the key to dissemination of the US legal model. Unlike case law, the guidelines could be easily transmitted and explained to national or legal outsiders.

According to the EEOC guidelines,[9] for sexual harassment to be illegal as a type of sex discrimination, it needs to be behavior of a sexual nature and unwelcome. MacKinnon's two main types of harassment were defined in the 1980 Guidelines: quid pro quo in (1) and (2) below, and hostile environment in (3) below. The guidelines stated in part:

> Unwelcome sexual advances, requests for sexual favors, and other verbal or physical conduct of a sexual nature constitute sexual harassment when
>
> (1) submission to such conduct is made either explicitly or implicitly a term or condition of an individual's employment,
>
> (2) submission to or rejection of such conduct by an individual is used as the basis for employment decisions affecting such individual, or
>
> (3) such conduct has the purpose or effect of substantially interfering with an individual's work performance or creating an intimidating, hostile, or offensive working environment.

Six years later, in the first major decision on sexual harassment, the US Supreme Court relied heavily on the EEOC guidelines, and MacKinnon's original argument, in fashioning their opinion. The legal form of sexual harassment had now been imprinted on the domestic and international legal conscious. The EEOC guidelines acted as a legal form book for the international debates to follow.

The Rise of Sexual Harassment Law in Austria

Compared to the USA, sexual harassment law was a late arrival to Austria. The prohibition on sexual harassment in employment (*Sexuelle Belästigung am Arbeitsplatz*) was included as a type of 'discrimination' in the Austrian Equal Treatment Act in 1992, 13 years after the original Act (*Gleichbehandlungsgesetz*, or GBG).[10] Austria is a civil law country and based on statutory law. This is in contrast to the US system of case law, which is based on both statutory law and judicial interpretation of statutory and non-statutory law. In Austria, it is the Equal Treatment Statute and accompanying motives, rather than individual cases, that provide the primary basis for judicial decision making. Thus, the legal protection of sexual harassment could not develop through case law, as it did in the USA, but must occur through the political system in the form of new legislation. This means that, to create a new legal protection, a new law must be passed. One might wonder if a 'sexual harassment law' could have been passed and signed in 1986 in the USA, the year of the Supreme Court decision in *Meritor Savings Bank* v. *Vinson*, 477 U.S. 57, 106 S.Ct. 2399, 91 L.Ed.2d 49 (1986)(hereinafter *Vinson*) by then President Ronald Reagan.

Unlike US law, Austria's sexual harassment statute theoretically covers all possible instances of sexual harassment. A decision by one court has no bearing on a later decision with similar facts. Each new case can, theoretically, be answered by the statute or its accompanying motives. But as a matter of practice, earlier cases are often used by judges in understanding how to apply the law, and are used by lawyers in making their arguments to the judge. Unlike the US system of common law, however, these cases do not hold formal precedential value and judges are not bound by earlier decisions.

Even given these differences in the context of the US and Austrian legal systems, feminists and activists in Austria relied on the research and law from the USA in establishing an Austrian law of sexual harassment. In addition to invoking the USA in support for sexual harassment law, the main text is virtually indistinguishable from the EEOC guidelines.[11] This is particularly fascinating considering the quirk in US sexual harassment law: it is defined by case law under a statute passed with its primary emphasis on ending racial discrimination in the workplace. The way the Austrian sexual harassment law came to be is a fascinating story, and it begins with Austria's recent political history.

Austria regained full sovereignty ten years after the end of World War II. There is much debate within and outside Austria about the meaning of the events leading up to and after Austria's non-military acquisition and eventual annexation by Nazi Germany in 1938. Many in Austria refer to the Nazi occupation and point to the demise of the Austrian state and the influx of 100 000 German soldiers and 16 000 policemen into Austria beginning on 12 March 1938 as proof that the Austrians were Hitler's first victims (Holzer, 1998). Others inside and outside Austria assert that Austria was Nazi Germany's willing accomplice and that, while many Austrians perished at the hands of Nazi Germany, many more supported the regime. As described by Rickett (1966; 1994: 147), 'On 12 March [1938] the German army was on its way and Hitler had got as far as Linz in its wake. The next day he entered Vienna, with the Gestapo of course, amid scenes of delirious enthusiasm, especially from the unemployed.'

As part of the German Reich, Vienna was captured by the Russians in 1945 and occupied by the American, French, English and Soviet allied forces until 1955. Austria maintained its politically ambiguous status even after the end of World War II. Geographically and politically nested between Western Germany, Switzerland and Italy, on the political west, and the former Yugoslavia and Czechoslovakia and Hungary on the Soviet side, Austria chose the special position of 'permanent neutrality', between the Soviets and the West as a way out of the quartered allied occupation (Kennedy and Specht, 1990).

The Second Republic of Austria has been governed by relatively stable coalitions between the Social Democrats (Socialists) and the People's Party (also called the Christian Democrats). Although the Socialists briefly aligned with the right-wing Freedom Party from 1983 to 1986, there were relatively stable coalition governments in Austria until 1994 – just as Austria was preparing to enter the European Union. The early 1990s were difficult for Austria's political identity, since the special status of 'neutrality' was faltering after the success of Gorbachev's *perestroika* and the fall of the Berlin Wall. In 1994, 66.3 per cent of voters agreed to join the European Union, further challenging the concept of neutrality (Appelt, 1998). That same year marked the rise of the Freedom Party under the leadership of Jörg Haider and, today, the Freedom Party is part of the ruling coalition.

Yet this instability is new to post-World War II Austria. In addition to a stable coalition for many years, there has also been relative stability in labor and management relations. A key component of Austria's postwar political culture in the neutral Second Republic has been the role of the social partners (*Sozialpartnerschaft*), which formalize cooperation among the government, industry, workers and unions in economic decision making (Gilbert, 1987). It was in this context, and under the leadership of a Socialist-led coalition government, that feminists successfully achieved amendments to the conservative Family Act, the passage of the Equal Treatment Law and, eventually, the adoption of a sexual harassment provision.

The Austrian women's movement gained momentum in the 1970s both within the Social Democratic Party and independent of the party (Appelt, 1998). Under Socialist Party leadership between 1979 and 1983, six of 22 cabinet members were female (Rosenberger, 1998). Feminists also had a friend in the Austrian Federation of Trade Unions. As Appelt describes, unions included in their primary goals the 'safeguarding, the improvement and the consolidation of the protection of women and youth workers by legal acts' (1998: 89). However, the work of the unions and the Socialist Party for women's rights should not be overstated. While unions and the Socialist Party actively promoted women's rights, they were both very much internally male-dominated (Appelt, 1998; Rosenberger, 1998). As described by Appelt (1998: 89), 'We can characterize the Austrian federation of unions as a male-dominated organization with a small niche for women'.

Nevertheless, the Austrian independent women's movement and women's groups affiliated with the Socialist Party pushed for reproductive rights and rights within family life. In 1974, the predominantly Catholic Austria legalized abortion in the first trimester. The following year, Parliament revised the Family Act. As Rosenberger (1998: 110) comments, this was the 'beginning of policies supporting gender equality'. The Family Act, dating from 1811, legally reiterated the conservative social norm of 'the father as the head of the family' (ibid.: 108). Parliament amended the law stressing partnership and the joint rights and responsibilities of a husband and wife. Among other things, the amendments did away with the requirement that a wife obtain the permission of her husband in order to work (Rosenberger, 1998). The next major women's rights legislation in Austria was soon to follow.

The 1979 Equal Treatment Act prohibited discrimination in the salaries of men and women.[12] Although only weakly defined as 'disadvantageous differentiation which is undertaken without material justification' (ibid.: 113) the Act uses the term 'discrimination' to reflect the social problems it purports to address. This discrimination terminology was carried through to the sexual harassment provision (when it was added in 1992). The use of the concept of discrimination makes Austrian law more like the US legal context, but, as I will soon discuss, distinguishes it from the European Union.

The 1979 Equal Treatment Act also established an Equal Treatment Commission (GBK)[13] to hear claims and make non-binding recommendations under the statute. By law, the Commission consists of representatives of Austrian unions, industry and government (the 'social partners'). Without the enforcement powers of the courts, the opinions[14] of the Commission are treated as suggestions or proposals, rather than enforceable legal decisions.

That same year, the socialist government set up two government offices to address the feminist agenda: a general women's affairs office (which later became the Ministry of Women's Affairs in 1990) and another office for the affairs of working women (Rosenberger, 1998). Although the office for working women was dismantled during the short-lived Socialist and Freedom Party coalition, in 1983, Johanna Dohnal, the appointed Secretary for General Women's Affairs, was a key figure in the passage of Austrian sexual harassment law. Until she was abruptly fired in 1995, just before the Beijing International Woman's Conference, Minister Dohnal worked inside the Austrian government for women's rights and especially for a sexual harassment law.

In 1985, the Equal Treatment Law was strengthened to increase its jurisdiction, requiring equality in vocational training, fringe benefits and gender-neutral job advertising. It also limited state subsidies to those companies in compliance with the Act (ibid.). Despite the strengthening of the Equal Treatment Act, women's groups were critical of it because they believed that, while women might be equal on paper, they were, in practice, unequal (ibid.). Nevertheless, the issue of sexual harassment was rising strongly within the trade unions. Trade union staff representatives were faced with the problems of sexual harassment (within companies) and they knew first-hand of the sexual harassment working women faced. In response to the rising importance of sexual harassment to working women in Austria, feminists within the trade unions raised the issue internally and began generating discussions of sexual harassment in Austria. They were eventually approached by the office of the

Ministry for Labor and Social Affairs about disseminating surveys for a study they intended to conduct.[15]

In 1986, the Women's Office of the Ministry for Labor and Social Affairs commissioned a study on sexual harassment in the workplace: *Sexuelle Belästigung am Arbeitsplatz* (Hopfgartner and Zeichen, 1988). This was the first major study of sexual harassment in Austria and is certainly the most well-known study today (Zippel, 1999). It was designed to examine the prevalence of sexual harassment in the workplace, and the impact that sexual harassment has on women's lives.

The authors of *Sexuelle Belästigung am Arbeitsplatz* in the Women's Office in the Ministry for Labor and Social Affairs presented their findings by invoking international law and research on sexual harassment. Much of this law and research came from the USA. Along with a 1983 definition by the Health and Research Employees Association of Australia, and the United Kingdom's 'The Charter for Equality for Women Within Trade Unions' (TUC), the authors' reference law and research focused on the USA. All of these English-language texts remained true to the original EEOC guidelines in the USA.

The international legal model of sexual harassment in the late 1980s was the US EEOC model (in whatever guise), just as the USA was the source of most of the available research on sexual harassment. As Collins (1996: 25) observed,

> In 1980, few people in Europe discussed sexual harassment as a problem; it did not have a name, and those subjected to it had no legal protection. By contrast, in the United States, discussion on the nature of the problem and ways to deal with it had begun in the 1970s. By the decade's close, activists on both sides of the Atlantic were aware that the Equal Employment Opportunities Commission had developed guidelines and a legal position on what constituted sexual harassment.

Hofpgartner and Zeichen reviewed the EEOC Guidelines on sexual harassment, research from the Merit Systems Protection Board study, Catherine MacKinnon's *Sexual Harassment of Working Women*, Lin Farley's *Sexual Shakedown* and the Working Women's Institute publications, as well as the research of US academics such as Barbara Gutek, Marilyn Brewer, Joy Livingston, Sandra Tangri and others, in their study.

The Hopfgartner and Zeichen (1988) study showcases the US *Redbook Magazine* study that found over 90 per cent of women had been sexually harassed (Collins and Blodgett, 1981). Their own study shares that study's problem of unrepresentative sampling, although it is equally dramatic in its findings. Hofpgartner and Zeichen found that, in Austria, 81 per cent of women in their study had been sexually harassed. More recent studies indicate lower percentages (see Zippel, 1999). Hopfgartner and Zeichen's study was grand in design but, of the 10 000 questionnaires sent to labor unions for distribution, only 14 per cent were returned. The findings were used prominently in the political debate over the inclusion of sexual harassment in the Equal Treatment Law. While the methodology of this study is certainly suspect, like the *Redbook Magazine* study in the USA, Hopfgartner and Zeichen's findings were important in establishing sexual harassment as a problem of *Austrian* women, although they did this by citing the problem as one that is recognized and researched outside Austria. This study set the stage for the debates over sexual harassment still to come. Austrian sexual harassment law was adopted within an international context.

Sexual harassment was also becoming an issue of the International Labour Organization (of the United Nations). However, it was not until 1988 that the ILO publicly raised the issue of sexual harassment (Aeberhard-Hodges, 1996). When they did so, the Committee of Experts listed examples of sexual harassment that are unwelcome, and associated with the conditions of employment (that is, salary, promotion) (ibid.). These standards are also evident in the EEOC guidelines. This and other, more minor, initiatives of the ILO regarding sexual harassment, were not disseminated broadly in the 1980s but, because of the reporting requirement of the ILO, government officials in Austria knew it was a rising issue of international concern.

The year 1990 was an important one for the Equal Treatment Act in Austria. The law was once again amended to prohibit sex discrimination in the working relationship and in job dismissal. These amendments also established an '*Anwältin für Gleichbehandlungsfragen*', or a state-subsidized lawyer,[16] to assist plaintiffs with equal treatment claims and to facilitate conciliation between employers and employees regarding equal treatment violations before the Equal Treatment Commission. However, it was a ruling by the Constitutional Court (*Verfassungsgericht*) that mobilized women's rights activists and eventually led to the adoption of a sexual harassment provision two years later.

After several failed attempts to overturn it, the gender-specific retirement age for state benefits was finally struck down by the Constitutional Court as a violation of Equal Treatment Law. No longer could women retire at an earlier age than men. This meant that Parliament would have to amend the law and provide equality in retirement ages. Proponents of women's rights took this legislative opportunity to demand the long-touted de facto equality, which included the rising issue of sexual harassment. In response to the impending change in the retirement ages, the Minister of Women's Affairs, Johanna Dohnal, and other women politicians presented a list of equality demands to the government and industry that included workplace equality. The demand for a sexual harassment provision was high on their list.

As the 'package of equality', as it would come to be known, was debated within Austria, the government was formulating its post-cold war future. The

Equal Treatment negotiations occurred against the backdrop of a declining Soviet Union and strengthening European Union. A 1991 article by Hugo Schally, entitled 'Austria and the Central European Countries', describes the dramatic political and economic shifts in the region at the time:

> Europe, a continent which only a few years ago seemed to be frozen in time, is presently experiencing a complete and dramatic change of history. As the present events bring Europe back into the international spotlight, the bipolar system of the postwar era is about to be replaced by multipolarism . . . Since 1986 two previously unimaginable developments have changed the course of events in Europe. The first of these developments is the European Community's attempt to create a single European market. The second is the end of Communist domination in the Eastern European Countries. (Schally, 1991: 267–8)

Austrian participation in the European Union was not something to be taken lightly. Joining the European Union would mean legislative conformity in accordance with the laws of the European Union. Kennedy and Specht (1990: 409) warned Austria that

> joining the European Communities means a large-scale and largely irreversible transformation of a state's substantive law, governmental structure and international status. . . . Membership would so dramatically transform both the constitutional structure of Austrian government and its legal capacity for an independent defense that Austria's international legal status as a 'permanent neutral' would be jeopardized.

In addition to concerns about giving up 'neutrality', Austrians were also concerned about joining a European Union controlled by their larger and more economically powerful neighbor, Germany. As Judt (1998: 135) describes it, 'Austrians no longer seek an Anschluß [the German/Austrian unification of World War II] – indeed, many of them fear absorption into a German-dominated Europe – but Germany is always on their minds, whereas Austria is a topic of almost no sustained interest in Germany itself.' Similarly, Holzer (1998: 148) in a criticism of Judt, makes this point:

> True, Germany plays a very important role, both in real terms and in the memory of many Austrians. Many have retained a partly fearful, partly jealous, partly self-righteous inferiority complex. The benign neglect of Austria by many Germans, the imbalance in degree of mutual attention, is, however, quite normal between neighbors of such disproportionate size and power.

Given Austria's history, geography and culture, as reflected by Judt and Holzer, even if economic pragmatism demanded the joining of the European Union, it would not be without concern about their northern neighbor.

It was within this context – the end of the cold war, the rising importance of the European Union and concerns about a strong Germany – that industry, union and government leaders in Austria eventually supported sexual harassment legislation. While the issue of sexual harassment had been raised before by Austrian feminists in government and the trade unions, until this point it was strongly resisted by industry leaders and many in government. However, these same leaders of industry generally supported joining the EU, and used the negotiations over the Equal Treatment Act to do two things. First, they agreed to a sexual harassment law that they believed they would eventually be subject to anyway – under EU law; second, they voluntarily adopted their own law, in their own manner, before Germany.[17]

While the EU has not issued a *mandatory* requirement that member states have a specific prohibition against sexual harassment during the equal treatment negotiations, at the time of the Equal Treatment negotiations, it looked as though a sexual harassment directive was likely to be adopted by the EU. Although this was not to be the case, the Austrian industry representatives who were negotiating the equal treatment domestically were also hopeful partners in an EU that had several equality policies. From its inception in the Treaty of Rome 1957, the EU has supported equal treatment between men and women with directives and action programs (Collins, 1996).

The issue of sexual harassment was first addressed by the EU in the context of the Equal Treatment Directive. In 1976, the European Council of Ministers passed this directive outlawing sex discrimination at work and in worker training. While making no mention of the concept of sexual harassment, it set the stage for legal arguments to come (Carter, 1992; McCrudden, 1993; Earle and Madek, 1993; Webb, 1994; Bernstein, 1994).[18] At the turn of the decade, sexual harassment was a major feminist issue in the USA and one that was beginning to receive greater attention on the continent. In 1983, an industrial tribunal in the UK decided the issue of sexual harassment in favor of a female apprentice in a car mechanic shop in Northern Ireland (Collins, 1996).[19] The tribunal found that her treatment constituted unlawful discrimination and this led to mounting pressure 'for a Union-wide response to the problem' (ibid.: 26).

Voluntary measures in the 1980s followed the Equal Treatment Directive. First, in 1984, the Council of Ministers passed a resolution calling for 'dignity for women at the workplace' and for action policies to eliminate inequalities affecting women.[20] The EU took two more steps in 1986, the year of the *Vinson* decision in the USA. First, the European Commission agreed to the request of the Council of Ministers on Women's Issues and began to research the issue of sexual harassment in the European communities (Collins, 1996). This resulted in a widely-cited study on sexual harassment in the European communities by Michael Rubenstein, and his recommendation for an EU directive on sexual harassment.

Finally, in 1990, the year the equal treatment negotiations began in Austria, the Council of Ministers addressed sexual harassment directly, calling for the protection of the dignity of men and women at work in a resolution.[21] The resolution defined sexual harassment, under some circumstances, as contrary to the principle of equal treatment, already the subject of an EU directive (Carter, 1992). Soon after, a recommendation and Code of Practice were enacted which further elaborated the legal meaning of sexual harassment and it called on member states to pursue measures aimed at creating a climate of respect for men and women in the workplace, explicitly stating that sexual harassment is contrary to the already existing Equal Treatment Directive.[22] The EU definition of sexual harassment relied greatly on the EEOC guidelines for the legal structure, even though it was in the context of 'dignity' of the worker rather than anti-discrimination, reflecting the economic context of the EU and existing categories within labor law. Like US law, the recommendation did not provide specific examples of behavior considered sexual harassment, and initiatives to do so were quickly killed in the consultation process (Collins, 1996). Instead, the recommendation and Code of Practice used the broad EEOC formulation of quid pro quo and hostile environment sexual harassment. The EU defines sexual harassment as follows:

> (1) . . . conduct of a sexual nature, or other conduct based on sex affecting the dignity of women and men at work, including conduct of superiors and colleagues, constitutes an intolerable violation of the dignity of workers or trainees and is unacceptable if:
>
> (a.) such conduct is unwanted, unreasonable and offensive to the recipient;
> (b.) a person's rejection of, or submission to, such conduct on the part of employers or workers (including superiors or colleagues) is used explicitly or implicitly as a basis for a decision which affects that person's access to vocational training, access to employment, continued employment, promotion, salary or any other employment decisions;
>
> and/or
>
> (c.) such conduct creates an intimidating, hostile or humiliating working environment for the recipient.[23]

It is also important to note that the EU recommendation retained the USA's model of hostile environment sexual harassment among co-workers. In Spanish and Swedish sexual harassment law, both adopted under socialist-led governments, co-worker sexual harassment was not explicitly covered (Valiente, 2000; Elman, 2000). Valiente (2000) argues that this is likely the product of the socialist political ideology.

While the recommendation and Code of Practice do not place a *mandatory* obligation on the part of member states to pass national legislation conforming to the recommendation, as would a directive, they do have some legal power

(Carter, 1992; McCrudden, 1993). In *Grimaldi* v. *Fonds de Maladies Professionnelles* (Case 322/88 [1990] IRLR 400), the European Court of Justice ruled in 1990 on the role of recommendations in the national courts of member states (Collins, 1996). Though neither the recommendation, resolutions nor the Code of Practice are binding on member states, the European Court of Justice ruled that national courts must use recommendations to clarify or supplement the binding measures of the EU, such as directives (ibid.). This means that the recommendation on sexual harassment can be used by plaintiffs in national courts to argue that the Equal Treatment Directive of the EU covers sexual harassment.

After two years of negotiations resulting from a ruling on unequal retirement ages, the Austrian 'Equal Treatment Package' was adopted. It included the provision on sexual harassment long sought by women's rights activists in Austria.[24] Reflecting the concern about how Austria would appear to an EU that Austrian industry wanted to join, one Austrian representative of industry who participated in the negotiations described the 'voluntariness' of the provision. But, he added, 'we have our peace in Brussels [the headquarters of the European Union] in this field. We wouldn't have it, still having a law without a sexual harassment paragraph.'[25] Explaining the passage of the sexual harassment provision, another government official also involved in the negotiations explained why they supported the sexual harassment provision: 'First thing, it was mostly to comply with the [EU] and second, [it was] to show that they supported woman's wishes in this respect.'[26] While women's rights activists assert that a sexual harassment provision would have been passed even without the EU umbrella, and point to the personal charisma of Johanna Dohnal in achieving legislative success, membership of the EU was, at the very least, a catalyst accelerating the agreement of industry and government. The Austrian law came into effect on 1 January 1993, over a year before Germany legislated on the issue of sexual harassment in the Employee Protection Act.[27]

The Austrian law is clearly modeled on the US EEOC definition of sexual harassment (and MacKinnon's original conceptualization) as well as the EU's, whose own roots are in the early US conceptualization. At the national level of social context, we see that a combination of activism and legal imagination in the USA led to the recognition of sexual harassment as a legal wrong. While essentially a domestic issue in the USA, sexual harassment law in Austria was adopted within an international political and legal context.

In the next chapter, I review the law of sexual harassment in the USA and Austria, focusing on their similarities.

Notes

1 Sexual harassment claims based on Title VII are affected by the limitations of the statute. Importantly, the term 'employer', under the the statute, is restricted to those employing 15 or more employees. Title VII of the Civil Rights Act of 1964 also exempts Congress, Native American tribes, private membership clubs and religious groups. Some state laws define the employers covered by sex discrimination law more expansively. In addition, the statute requires plaintiffs to file prior to the expiration of the statute of limitations, which is 180 days after the sexual harassment occurred (42 U.S.C. Sec. 2000e-5(e)(1988)).
2 13 Fair Empl. Prac. Cas. (BNA) 123 (D.D.C) 1974.
3 568 F.2d 1044 (3rd Cir. 1977).
4 *Barnes* v. *Costle*, 561 F.2d 983 (D.C. Cir. 1977).
5 *Garber* v. *Saxon Business Products*, 552 F.2d 10132 (4th Cir. 1977); *Tomkins* v. *Public Service Electric and Gas Co.*, 568 F.2d 1044 (3rd Cir. 1977).
6 Other studies with more reliable sampling methods have found that about one-half of working women experience some type of sexual harassment at work (United States Merit Systems Protection Board, 1981; Gutek, 1985; Fitzgerald and Shullman, 1993; Boiarsky *et al.*, 1995; Griffin-Shelley, 1985) with somewhat higher rates for women in predominantly male workplaces (Gruber, 1998). In an analysis of the results of 18 studies, Gruber estimates that 44 per cent of women have been sexually harassed, although the range extends from 28 to 75 per cent (Gruber, 1990).
7 Weeks *et al.* examined the period between 1970 and 1982.
8 As held in *EEOC* v. *Arabian Am. Oil Co.*, the EEOC's interpretations of Title VII are persuasive but not controlling. The Supreme Court has held that they are to be used when construing ambiguous terms. See *Vogel* v. *City of Cincinnati*, 959 F.2d at 594, 598 (6th Cir.) Cert denied, 113 S.Ct. 86 (1992); *Fray* v. *Omaha World Herald Co.*, 960 F.2d 1370, 1377 (8th Cir. 1992); or, for guidance, *Meritor Savings Bank* v. *Vinson*, 477 U.S. 57, 106 S.Ct. 2399, 91 L.Ed.2d 49 (1986) (hereinafter *Vinson*) at 65. In the most recent cases of sexual harassment before the Supreme Court, the Court relied heavily on the EEOC guidelines (for example, *Faragher* v. *City of Boca Raton*, 118 S.Ct., 2275 (1998); *Burlington Industries, Inc.* v. *Ellerth*, 118 S.Ct. 2257 (1998)).
9 29 C.F.R. 1604.11 (1980).
10 *Gleichbehandlungsgesetz* BGBI Nr 108/1979, idF BGBI Nr 290/1985, 410/1990 and 833/1992.
11 These similarities are also seen in the European Union definition, although the EU primarily relies on the frame of worker dignity, rather than discrimination. Austria uses both the conceptions of discrimination and dignity in its law.
12 GBG sec. 2(2). The law at this point only included private employers.
13 *Gleichbehanglungskomission* (hereinafter referred to as GBK) sec. 3(1)–(6) and secs 4–6.
14 Written opinions resulting from Equal Treatment Commission cases are not entitled 'Bescheid' or 'decision', as are court opinions; rather, they are entitled *Vorschlag*, meaning a suggestion or a proposal.
15 Personal communication with trade union official, RLA021597.
16 GBG sec. 3a(1)–(6). The 'in' ending in the German language connotes that the individual is female. Thus the lawyer for equal treatment questions is described as a female lawyer in the statute. The statute provides for this lawyer to act as an advocate before the GBK on behalf of those claiming violations of the law and as an ombudsman between employers and employees claiming violations of the equal treatment law.
17 For a comparison of German sexual harassment law, see Zippel (2000). Also see Valiente

(1998; 2000) for a discussion of Spain's 1989 adoption of a sexual harassment law – the first in the European Union – and Elman (1996a; 1996b; 2000) for a discussion of Sweden's sexual harassment law.

18 Directive 76/207, 1976 OJ (L 39/40).

19 *M* v. *Crescent Garage Ltd*, IT Case 23/83/SD.

20 Council Recommendation of 31 December 1984 on the Promotion of Positive Action for Women, 33 O.J. Eur. Comm. (No. L311) (1984) (Council Directive 84/635/EEC).

21 Council Resolution of 29 May 1990 on the Protection of the Dignity of Women and Men at Work, 33 O.J. Eur. Comm. (No. C157) (1990). In addition, the Code of Practice recognizes sexual harassment as 'contrary to the principle of equal treatment' under the 1976 directive, meaning that sexual harassment may be actionable under a member nation's Equal Treatment Law that does not specifically mention sexual harassment (Earle and Madek, 1993: 87, footnote 325).

22 Commission Recommendation of 27 November 1991 on the Protection of the Dignity of Women and Men at Work (O.J. C (91) 2625).

23 1990 OJ 157, cited in Earle and Madek (1993: 76).

24 GBG sec. 12. The package also included extension of paid leave for a relative's illness and shifted the focus of discrimination under that statute from equal pay to comparable worth (Rosenberger, 1998). In 1993, an affirmative action program for women was instituted, although two years later is was rejected by the European Supreme Court (ibid.; Decision of the European Supreme Court of 17 October 1995, Nr. C-450/93 related to Provision 177 EC-Treaty). A provision subjecting federal employees to an Equal Treatment Law was eventually required for conformity to the laws of the EU. This came in 1993 and provided for a federal Equal Treatment Law and Commission.

25 Personal communication, RLA032596A:16.

26 Personal communication, RLA0321962A:2.

27 For a comparison of US and German law, see Zippel (2000b).

3 Sexual Harassment Law in the USA and Austria

Introduction

Although sexual harassment law is well known, the legal boundaries of what is illegal and legal are relatively ambiguous. Sexual harassment law, like many other laws, is riddled with ambiguities. While everyone knows sexual harassment is illegal, what exactly is sexual harassment? Rather than a concrete act, such as murder, theft or rape, much law only vaguely defines illegal conduct. The laws of both the United States and Austria have shied away from providing 'stiff behavior typologies' (Bei and Novak, 1997: 124; Mensch, 1998[1]), but this also means that standards of illegality are difficult to ascertain.

While the underlying principle of ambiguity in law may be to allow for changing social norms or conditions, it creates a puzzle both for individuals regulated by ambiguous law and for the regulators of illegal conduct. In this chapter, I review the definitions of the legal harm of sexual harassment in the USA and Austria, but I also recognize, and indeed argue, that the 'law' and its perception or implementation are only tenuously related.

The legal definition of sexual harassment in the USA and Austria shows the strong reliance on the US's EEOC definition of sexual harassment in both countries. The EEOC guidelines define sexual harassment in part as follows:[2]

> Unwelcome sexual advances, requests for sexual favors, and other verbal or physical conduct of a sexual nature constitute sexual harassment when
>
> (Quid pro quo)
> (1) submission to such conduct is made either explicitly or implicitly a term or condition of an individual's employment,
> (2) submission to or rejection of such conduct by an individual is used as the basis for employment decisions affecting such individual, or
>
> (Hostile Environment) (3) such conduct has the purpose or effect of unreasonably interfering with an individual's work performance or creating an intimidating, hostile, or offensive working environment.

Once sexual harassment in the USA was recognized as a legal wrong, the core legal definition of sexual harassment was established quickly, and has changed little since it was first drafted. This legal definition of sexual harassment does little to help individuals categorize particular conduct as illegal or legal. Despite these clear problems, an ocean away, Austrian representatives of government, industry and labor relied on these definitions in drafting their own sexual harassment law. Sexual harassment law's rapid dissemination was due to the activism of feminists in national politics, but it was also likely due to its legal form. First, sexual harassment fits easily into economic arguments. Indeed, in its legal incarnation, it is a result of the employment relationship. Although empirical data on this are sparse, prohibiting sexual harassment might easily be characterized as a way to save organizations money in employee absenteeism, turnover and lost productivity. Second, sexual harassment fits well into patriarchal notions about protecting the chastity of women from sexual predators. While far different from the context of Catherine MacKinnon's (1978) treatise, the protection of women by men from unwanted sexual advances is a strong undertone in both US and EU law.

Finally, the legal form that sexual harassment ultimately took made it initially appear as non-threatening to businesses. While I do not suggest that corporations wanted sexual harassment law, its broad ambiguity initially required little of US firms for compliance. Even with its ambiguities (or perhaps because of them), the US sexual harassment definition has been used as a legal model around the world today.

There are many similarities between the Austrian law and the European Union recommendation on sexual harassment. The EU's legal standard (derived in part, from the EEOC guidelines) had a marked influence on the text of Austria's law, and continues to have a formal role in the interpretation of sexual harassment claims. Seen in the context of the EU recommendation and the EEOC guidelines from the USA, the form of the Austrian sexual harassment law clearly shares the same substantive components. Translated from the German-language text of the Equal Treatment Act (GBG), the Austrian law states, in part:[3]

> Sec. 2(1 b). Sexual harassment arises when behavior of a sexual nature occurs that reduces a person's dignity, is unwelcome, uninvited or offensive and
>
> > (1) creates a timid, hostile or humiliating work environment for the afflicted person,[4] (2) That the person concerned bears or refuses behavior of a sexual nature from the employer, superior or colleague and then is made the basis (openly or silently) for a decision with a disadvantageous impact on the access of that person to professional training, employment, continuing employment, promotion, or remuneration or for any other disadvantageous decision concerning the working relationship.

US and Austrian Sexual Harassment Law

The Basic Definition

While there are some differences in application of the definition, the laws are striking in their similarities. Like US law, the logic of Austrian law places sexual harassment within the context of anti-discrimination and formally includes cases brought by both women and men (Bei and Novack, 1997). However, US sexual harassment law is older and more elaborated than Austrian sexual harassment law, which came into effect in 1993.

In the USA, the first Supreme Court case addressing the issue of sexual harassment under civil rights law was *Meritor Savings Bank* v. *Vinson*, 477 U.S. 57, 106 S.Ct. 2399 (1986) (hereinafter *Vinson*). In this case, Mechelle Vinson brought a claim of sexual harassment against her supervisor and the bank after she was discharged for excessive use of sick leave. Vinson stated that she was frequently asked during and after business hours to engage in sexual relations with her supervisor. In fear of losing her job, Vinson testified that she agreed to some of the sexual encounters with her supervisor and was raped on others, as well as being fondled by her supervisor in the presence of other employees (*Vinson*, at 2402). In this case, a unanimous court, the justices defined two types of actionable sexual harassment according to the EEOC guidelines: quid pro quo or hostile environment.

In the *Vinson* decision, the court also relied on the EEOC 'welcomeness' standard (as opposed to a voluntariness standard) and defined sexual harassment as 'Unwelcome sexual advances, requests for sexual favors, and other verbal or physical conduct of a sexual nature' (*Vinson*, at 66). The concept of welcomeness is important to sexual harassment law in both the USA and Austria because it provides an exclusion for mutually desired flirting and dating at work. Determining welcomeness often turns on observable aspects of the victim's behavior, such as the victim's manner, dress, past sexual relationships with the defendant or participation in telling sexual stories and jokes at work.[5] Of course, deciding if something is mutually desired, or welcome, takes place in law after the victim has complained that it was not. It is not only unclear in law how victims would successfully express unwelcomeness; it is also unclear whether the victim's actions in different circumstances might override that expression. This basic definition of illegal sexual harassment today remains largely unchanged.

Types of Sexual Harassment

Both legal systems make a similar conceptual distinction in sexual harassment law between the two main types of sexual harassment, *quid pro quo* harassment and *hostile environment* harassment, and US courts continue to distinguish between them. *Quid pro quo* harassment involves 'the conditioning of concrete employment benefits on sexual favors' (*Vinson*, at 2403). As explained by Bei and Novak (1997: 127) in relation to the Austrian law, this is behavior 'that typically includes the promise of [employment] advantages for the tolerance, as well as the threatening of [employment] disadvantages on the rejection of sexual acts'. For example, *quid pro quo* harassment would include the situation where an employer demands sex from an employee, threatening the loss of the employee's job. It would still be considered sexual harassment whether or not the employee submitted to the demands, assuming the other conditions of a sexual harassment case were met. In *quid pro quo* harassment, tangible employment benefits, such as salary, promotions or evaluations, are based on sexual submission or refusal. While the early sexual harassment cases in the USA, such as *Barnes* v. *Costle*, 561 F.2d 983 (D.C. Cir. 1977) tended to fit this category, today almost all federal cases involve a claim of hostile environment sexual harassment.

Sexual harassment of this type creates a hostile or abusive work environment for the victim. It is similarly defined in Austrian law as behavior that 'creates an intimidating, hostile or humiliating work environment' (GBG Sec. 2(1b (1))). What does it take to cross the threshold of rude and annoying behavior to illegal conduct that is sexually harassing? The law is anything but clear. First described by the Supreme Court in *Vinson*, the definition of hostile environment sexual harassment was elaborated by the court in *Harris* v. *Forklift Systems, Inc*, 114 S.Ct. 367 (1993). In this case a unanimous court stated that the conduct contributing to a hostile environment must be 'severe' and 'pervasive',[6] but exactly *what* conduct that is can only be determined 'by looking at all of the circumstances'.[7] Austria's standard is equally ambiguous, requiring that the conduct (for any type of sexual harassment) impair personal dignity and affect the work atmosphere.[8]

Standards of Determining Sexual Harassment

Although *Harris* v. *Forklift Systems, Inc*, 510 U.S. 17, 22 (1993) was granted a Writ of Certiorari to the US Supreme Court on the narrow issue of damages,[9] the Supreme Court 'reaffirmed' the standard for determining a hostile work environment (*Harris*, at 126 L. Ed. 2d 295, 302) in this case. The court announced that a dual objective/subjective standard should be used to determine whether harassing conduct constitutes a hostile work environment. The conduct must be 'severe or pervasive enough to create an objectively hostile or abusive work environment – an environment that a reasonable person would find hostile or abusive' (ibid., at 302).

Thus the reasonable person test, used in many other areas of law, is also used as the standard to define a hostile work environment.[10] To do this, one must look at all of the circumstances, such as 'frequency of discriminatory conduct; its severity; whether it is physically threatening or humiliating, or a mere offensive utterance; and whether it unreasonably interferes with an employee's work performance' (ibid., at 302–3). The inclusion of the objective standard is seen as a check on oversensitive employees. This would theoretically limit sexual harassment to conduct in the normative extreme, but, like other aspects of sexual harassment law, the 'reasonable person standard' is quite ambiguous.

The second, *subjective* component of the test hinges on the victim's impressions of the experience. The victim must 'subjectively perceive the environment to be abusive' for a Title VII violation (ibid., at 37). This means that a theoretical 'tough victim' does not meet the legal requirements of a claim if she does not believe her work environment is abusive or hostile, even if a reasonable person would believe that it is. Alternatively, the theoretical 'oversensitive victim' who perceives her work environment as abusive or hostile would not meet the requirements of a claim unless a reasonable person would also perceive her work environment to be abusive and hostile. Thus, to meet the legal claim of hostile environment sexual harassment, the plaintiff must have both parts: the work environment must be objectively hostile or abusive and the victim must perceive the environment as hostile or abusive.

In Austria, in addition to the similar language of a hostile or humiliating work environment, the conduct must impair the personal dignity of the victim. You may recognize this standard from the EU, and as such it is interpreted through the duty of care an employer owes to the welfare of his or her employees (Bei and Novak, 1997: 124).[11] To meet the standard of sexual harassment, the behavior must be offensive to the victim (the subjective test).[12] To Bei and Novak, the crucial aspect in determining whether sexual harassment has occurred is 'whether the work atmosphere has become unbearable for the victim' (ibid.: 127). However, this is used in conjunction with generally acknowledged behavior standards (an objective standard). Bei and Novak (ibid.: 124) suggest that the 'examples of public acts such as whistling, unwelcome invitations to coffee or dinner are not sufficient enough to reach the standard of impairment of personal dignity'. They go on to suggest that 'physical contact that takes place against the will of the affected person, as well as the often mentioned "grabbing" fulfill the general requirements of this definition'.

The Sexual Nature Requirement

Another important aspect of sexual harassment law is the requirement that the conduct be *of a sexual nature*, although this appears to be more of an issue for scholars than it is an issue for courts. There is debate in US legal circles about whether sexual harassment is limited to only sexual harassment, or includes other aspects of gender harassment, as does the legal claim of racial harassment. Recent empirical examinations of sexual harassment find that individuals define three distinct types of sexual harassment: gender harassment, unwanted sexual attention and sexual coercion (for example, Gefand *et al.*, 1995; Fitzgerald and Hesson-McInnis, 1989).

Both the EEOC guidelines and the Austrian Equal Treatment Act stress that, to be considered sexual harassment in employment, conduct must be *of a sexual nature*. Sexually harassing conduct is most often, but not exclusively, reserved for things that take place in the sexual sphere (Schultz, 1998; Bei and Novak, 1997[13]). Determined only after the fact, there is particular ambiguity in categorizing behavior that includes both sexual and non-sexual elements (Schultz, 1998) and in determining whether the context of the conduct was sexual in nature.

In Austria, where there are far fewer scholarly debates or empirical examinations of the issue, it appears that, if the actionable conduct is not sexual in nature, judges interpret the statute to exclude that conduct. For example, an Austrian Labor Court determined that the comments directed at a female employee regarding her physical appearance were not sexual in nature, and therefore not sexual harassment.[14] It reasoned that, since only two of the seven questioned co-workers believed the jokes to be unpleasant, a violation of the victim's dignity or hostile work environment could not be established.

US courts appear to rule similarly. In their empirical study of all federal sexual harassment cases between 1986 and 1996, Juliano and Schwab (2000) found that plaintiffs who were alleging discriminatory but non-sexual behavior (devaluing language, belittling names and so on) were significantly less likely to win than plaintiffs alleging sexual or physical conduct. Further, while we might think of a hostile environment sexual harassment case as including an office with generally disparaging statements about women, posted pin-ups and graffiti, these types of sexual harassment cases are unlikely to be brought, and they are even more unlikely to win in US courts if they are brought. Almost all successful US sexual harassment cases involve conduct specific to the plaintiff, with or without general statements. The Juliano and Schwab (2000) study found that in just *four* of the hundreds of cases they studied, the plaintiffs alleged sexual comments about women in general. None of these claims was successful.

This empirical finding is in contrast to the notion in popular culture that it does not take much to create a workplace that is a hostile environment, and it does not take much to win a sexual harassment case. Indeed, exaggeration of the threat of individual rights-based lawsuits is common in US culture (Hayden,

1991). The belief in uneven plaintiff success is encouraged by uneven media reporting of plaintiff wins rather than defendant wins (Galanter, 1999; Epp, 1998b; McCann and Haltom, 1999). In contrast to perceptions that plaintiffs usually win, the Juliano and Schwab study (2000) found that plaintiffs won just over one-half of all federal court cases between 1986 and 1996. Other, less comprehensive studies showed even worse results for plaintiffs. For example, when examining the complaints formally made to the Illinois Department of Human Rights in 1981, Terpstra and Baker (1988) found that just 31 per cent received favorable outcome, with a mean award of $3234. Plaintiffs were more likely to win if the harassment was severe, if they had witnesses and if management was informed of the harassment. Moving the analysis to the federal courts, Terpstra and Baker found that plaintiffs won in 38 per cent of the cases (Terpstra and Baker, 1992).

Employer Liability

The issue of employer liability is an important one in sexual harassment cases. Because employers may be held liable for the sexual harassment of their employees, sexual harassment is an important organizational issue. However, while the possibility of liability looms large over employers, the probability is much more uncertain. Austrian law provides the same standard for all sexual harassment cases. The Austrian statute provides for a right for sexually harassed persons to be compensated by the harasser and by the employer where the employer knew of the harassment and upon notice failed to address it (Bei and Novak, 1997).[15] Employers are liable for their own harassing conduct and for 'culpably' failing to take remedial measures against the harassment of other employees or clients if the employer 'could not justifiably doubt the presence of sexual harassment' (ibid.: 128–9).[16] However, the law also receognizes that some types of remedial measures, such as dismissal, may not be available to the employer because of conflicting labor laws.

Under Austrian law, employers are directly responsible for their own conduct or for the conduct of others for whom they are legally responsible. The statute states:

> Sec. 2.(1a) Also, discrimination on the grounds of sex/gender arises, when, in connection with an employment relationship, an employee/worker
>
> 1. Is subject to, or the object of sexual harassment by the employer himself, or
>
> 2. The employer is guilty of not providing adequate remedy against sexual harassment by third parties where such remedies are provided for by law, under the norms of collective legal agreements or under the term of the employment contract.

Legal commentators and at least one Labor Court decision suggest employer liability for the actions of their CEO.[17] Another Labor Court case held the employer jointly liable for the sexual harassment of a manager.[18] However, many issues surrounding employer liability in Austria remain untested.[19]

In the USA, employer liability is much more complex. Courts treat employer liability differently, depending on the type of sexual harassment, the status of the harasser and whether the victim experiences 'tangible' damages. Because of a high degree of confusion in the lower courts over what legal standards define the circumstances of employer liability, the Supreme Court ruled on the issue in 1998. In two of the most recent Supreme Court cases, on the issue of employer liability the court clarified the standards for determining employer liability under US law.

The employing firm is directly responsible for quid pro quo harassment, if it is found to have occurred and threats are carried out (George, 1993; Barker and Haggard, 1992).[20] For quid pro quo harassment, and in cases where supervisors create a hostile environment that includes tangible employment action, such as 'discharge, demotion or undesirable reassignment', employers are vicariously liable for the actions of their supervisors[21] (*Faragher* v. *City of Boca Raton*, 1998 U.S. LEXIS 4216, 2320 (1998).

For other types of cases, the courts rely on preventive and corrective procedures implemented by the employer prior to substantive inquiry. In doing so, they draw heavily on the EEOC guidelines and existing trends in case law. There is a precursor to this holding in the 1991 EEOC 'Guidelines on Discrimination Because of Sex'.[22] In Section 1604.11.(f), the guidelines state:

> Prevention is the best tool for the elimination of sexual harassment. An employer should take all steps necessary to prevent sexual harassment from occurring, such as affirmatively raising the subject, expressing strong disapproval, developing appropriate sanctions, informing employees of their right to raise and how to raise the issue of harassment . . . and developing methods to sensitize all concerned.

In all but the most clear-cut (and rare) quid pro quo cases with tangible employment consequences, US courts are reluctant to hold employers liable if the employer has attempted to prevent sexual harassment or if the plaintiff has not given the employer an opportunity to address the sexual harassment dispute. When the hostile environment sexual harassment is created by co-workers, rather than supervisors, employers are only liable for sexual harassment under the broader negligence standard (used in Austria) when they know of the harassment and fail to take remedial measures addressing the harassment.[23] The difference here, between US and Austrian law, is that US law provides defensive benefits to employers who utilize procedures and policies preventively and remedially, while Austrian law focuses only on remedial action and does not specify sexual harassment policies as a legal defense.

When supervisors are involved in creating the hostile environment, the US law is more complex. In 1999, the Supreme Court ruled that, when the hostile environment is created by supervisors, but there is no tangible employment action (such as dismissal or a salary cut), the employer is still vicariously liable for the actions of its supervisors, but the employer can assert an affirmative defense. The affirmative defense has two components. First, employers must show that they 'exercised reasonable care to prevent and correct promptly any sexually harassing behavior'. This generally means that they have and disseminate a sexual harassment policy as well as providing an internal mechanism for claiming sexual harassment.[24] Second, employers must show that the victim 'unreasonably failed to take advantage of any preventive or corrective opportunities provided by the employer or to avoid harm otherwise' (*Faragher* v. *City of Boca Raton*, 1998 U.S. LEXIS 4216, 2320 (1998); also see *Burlington Industries Inc* v. *Kimberly Ellerth*, 1998 U.S. Lexis 4217 (1998)).[25] Plaintiffs are obligated to notify the organization and to try to resolve the dispute within the organization's specified procedures or they risk an affirmative defense in court.

Damages

Finally, US and Austrian law depart on the issue of damages. In the USA, the remedies for sexual harassment were extended beyond the traditional damages of equitable relief, such as an injunction to end the sexual harassment, back pay or reinstatement.[26] In 1991, Congress amended Title VII and included the possibility of compensatory and punitive damages in Title VII sexual harassment cases (Haney, 1993; Kandel, 1992).[27] The upward limits of these additional damages are capped and scaled, depending on the size of the employer.[28] The Civil Rights Act of 1991 also included the ability of a plaintiff to demand a jury trial when claiming compensatory or punitive damages, which was not available to sexual harassment plaintiffs before the Act. While the arsenal of potential damages is large, when plaintiffs win, the actual awards in sexual harassment cases are not exceptionally high. Juliano and Schwab's (1999) analysis revealed that the average award for a plaintiff win in federal district court sexual harassment cases was just $80 000. This amount is relatively low compared to other types of corporate claims.

Austrian law does not allow punitive damages but provides for actual damages and for damages for the 'loss of dignity', when there are no actual damages (GBG Sec. 2a.(7); Wilhelm, 1993).[29] This is estimated at a minimum 5000 Austrian Schillings (just under $500 in current values), and no maximum is statutorily provided.[30] While it is unique in Austrian law for individuals to be compensated for immaterial damages, this remedy for sexual harassment has been supported by legal commentary (Wilhelm, 1993) and in the first case of sexual harassment before the labor courts.[31]

Large plaintiff awards tend not to appear in sexual harassment claims, but appear as entitlement claims in unemployment or wrongful discharge disputes under the Austrian labor laws. There have been just a handful of sexual harassment cases actually heard in the Austrian courts. While the labor courts have been mostly successful forums for plaintiffs,[32] most of the formalized cases of sexual harassment in Austria go to the dispute facilitation forum of the Equal Treatment Commission, described in detail in the next section.

The Claims Process in the United States and Austria

The United States

Sexual harassment claims in US federal courts under Title VII of the 1964 Civil Rights Act must first be filed with the Equal Employment Opportunity Commission within 180 days[33] of the sexual harassment.[34] Because of some of the deficiencies in Title VII for victims of sexual harassment, some plaintiffs have turned to traditional tort claims, such as assault and battery, intrusion, negligent hiring and the intentional infliction of emotional distress, which generally do not cap remedies and have longer statute of limitations in which to bring suits (Korn, 1993). However, Title VII is the primary source of law for sexual harassment claims in the USA, and the focus of this inquiry.[35]

Originally, the EEOC was responsible for only Title VII cases, but today it is responsible for the enforcement of Title VII, the Age Discrimination in Employment Act and the Americans With Disabilities Act. Once a case is filed, the EEOC has 180 days to begin an investigation of the claim. At this point, a plaintiff may request a 'Notice of Right to Sue', without which the plaintiff does not have the legal authority to bring a private claim in federal court.

According to Selmi (1996), a right-to-sue notice is issued to about 25 per cent of the claimants without a completed investigation. If the EEOC investigates the claim, it makes an evaluation and at this point will dismiss the claim (finding no reasonable cause of action) or issue a cause finding. If the claim is dismissed, the EEOC provides a right-to-sue notice. The EEOC might also issue a cause finding. Acording to the Office of Research, Information and Planning of the EEOC, in fiscal year 1998, no reasonable cause was found in 42.3 per cent of the claims filed and resolved. Once a cause finding is issued, the Commission moves the case to non-binding conciliation.

If the case is not resolved, the EEOC may bring the case itself on behalf of the plaintiff, or issue a right-to-sue notice. According to the Office of Research, Information and Planning, in fiscal year 1998, the EEOC found reasonable cause in 6.1 per cent of the sexual harassment 'charges' filed and resolved. Of those, just 2.1 per cent were successfully conciliated (4 per cent did not reach resolution). Only rarely does the EEOC investigate sexual harassment and/or become the plaintiff in the case. For most plaintiffs, the EEOC is an administrative process requirement before going to federal court. Selmi (ibid.) reports that, in 1994, 83 per cent of the cases filed at the EEOC ended with the plaintiff requesting a right-to-sue notice. In the rare circumstances that the EEOC does bring the case, they provide the plaintiff with free legal assistance.

Most plaintiffs in sexual harassment cases, however, pay for their own lawyer either by contingency fee agreement or hourly payment. Almost all plaintiffs filing sexual harassment claims with the EEOC, and not excluded through administrative mistakes, bring their cases on their own, with a private attorney. Consider that the sexual harassment cases that go to the courts are the cases that were not settled internally, within the firm. This makes the cases we observe in court unusual (Galanter and Cahill, 1994): most cases where plaintiffs complain are born and die within the confines of the corporation.

Austria

From its inception, the Equal Treatment Act provided for an Equal Treatment Commission (GBK) (*Gleichbehandlungskommission*) to hear complaints under the law, including sexual harassment.[36] While sexual harassment claimants are not compelled to use the Commission, most cases that are filed go to the commission for resolution, rather than directly to the labor courts. Institutionally, the Commission is part of the Ministry for Women's Affairs in the Federal Chancellory, although it was formerly under the Minsitry for Social Affairs. The members of the Commission are reflective of Austria's highly respected 'social partnership' and chosen accordingly. The use of commissions comprising the Austrian social partners is not uncommon, especially for labor issues. The Commission is made up of 11 members, two of whom are appointed by government and two members each appointed by the two industry and two labor organizations in the Austrian social partnership.[37]

An employer, employee or an institution represented in the Commission, or the state-funded equal treatment lawyer can bring a case before the Commission.[38] The Commission then examines whether a violation of the GBG exists in that case.[39] Upon request the Commission states a professional opinion about the equal treatment decision which is to be published.[40] If the Commission decides that a violation of the Equal Treatment Law exists, it makes a proposal for compliance to the employer.[41] The respondent employer has one month within which to comply with the proposal.[42] If the employer fails to comply within one month, any party or institution represented on the Commission may sue the employer in civil court for enforcement; however, the courts are not compelled to follow the decisions of the Commission.[43]

The Commission has no enforcement powers, and if its verdicts are not complied with within one month, the claimant may sue for discrimination in court.[44] The decisions of the GBK are merely recommendations, or compromises. Thus, while a case may go before the Commission and end with a decision of sexual harassment, those found guilty of harassment have no obligation to provide a remedy other than what is voluntarily agreed. If the transgressor decides not to uphold his or her agreement, the Commission has no powers to enforce agreements made. Indeed, written opinions resulting from Commission cases are called 'Vorschlag' or 'suggestions', Court opinions; rather, are entitled 'Bescheid' or 'decisions'. However, they may be submitted to the court for review and may have some persuasive value, at the discretion of the judge: GBG at sec. 6(2–3).

In addition to the Equal Treatment Commission, Austrian law also provides for an equal treatment lawyer (*Gleichbehandlungsanwältin*).[45] Rather than being a neutral body, the equal treatment lawyer represents plaintiffs in claims under the Equal Treatment Law. She is nominated by the Ministry for Social Affairs 'for the consultation and support of persons who feel discriminated against in the sense of' the Equal Treatment Act. Her duties include appearing before the Commission with cases and conducting investigations on behalf of the commission.[46] Translated, her position is often described as an 'ombudsperson' (Bei and Novak, 1997).

Once a complaint is made to the equal treatment lawyer,[47] she has discovery powers to investigate and request information from those involved in the case, or potential witnesses.[48] If a violation of the law is suspected, the equal treatment lawyer then submits the case to the Commission.[49] In disputed cases, the equal treatment lawyer presents her case to the Commission. Claimants in these disputed cases can bring their own lawyer or are represented at no cost by the equal treatment lawyer.

In addition to the Equal Treatment Commission, sexual harassment plaintiffs can also go to the labor courts. Sexual harassment plaintiffs can seek legal assistance through the Chamber of Labor (*Arbeitskammer*), one component of the social partners with mandated membership for Austrian workers. The legal assistance provided by the Chamber of Labor is offered free for employees in organizations with five or more employees. While organizations have been generally supportive of sexual harassment claims and in educating workers as to the existence and meaning of sexual harassment, there have been some deviations in this support, especially in the western regions of Austria. While asistance with claims brought before the Labor Court may be free, this is not the case with the civil courts. This may be one reason why cases on sexual harassment have not been decided in the civil courts.

Free legal assistance from the Chamber of Labor may also be important in defending a suit by the employer for the Austrian equivalent of slander. Increasingly, Austrian employers have sued or threatened to sue victims claiming harassment for damage to their reputation (Bei and Novak, 1997: 43). The losing party must pay lawyer costs for themselves and for the prevailing party. While all such cases in Austria have been dismissed up to now, it is up to the regional Chamber of Labor[50] whether or not they will offer legal assistance to the defendant (the sexual harassment plaintiff). While it is important to those claiming sexual harassment, the Chamber of Labor's legal assistance is by no means certain and does not cover many of Austria's small-business employees owing to the minimum employee requirement.

The legal advantages to firms of adopting procedures for the resolution of sexual harassment disputes do not exist in Austria as they do in the USA. However, some employees, particularly employees of larger organizations, are represented by a union. Union representatives sometimes assist in resolving a dispute. This '*Betriebsrat*' is the official worker's representative in the company and is often the first to hear claims of sexual harassment. They are supported institutionally by the Federation of Trade Unions, which distributes educational material on sexual harassment law and provides information and training to individual *Betriebsrates*.

Sexual Harassment Law in Practice

While the formal legal systems of the US and Austria are different, most instances of sexual harassment in the workplace never involve courts or judges. Many lawsuits are settled by the parties before reaching a court decision. Other complaints are never presented in court. They are resolved within the organization, through a private disputing process such as mediation or arbitration. Still other complaints are resolved even more informally, within the organization. Some legal wrongs are never claimed because of fear of retribution (Prager *et al.*, 1996), difficulties associated with leaving the firm (Mahoney, 1992) or other sociopsychological reasons (Bumiller, 1987). Many other potential cases of sexual harassment are never even characterized by the victims as legal wrongs (Felstiner *et al.*, 1980). This suggests that we should turn to the place where sexual harassment is interpreted and implemented: the organization. The organizational context is a primary component of the social context role in shaping understandings of law. I now turn to the five organizational case studies that form the basis of this empirical study.

Notes

1 Seen in an historical perspective, Mensch suggests that, in the USA, 'the indeterminacy of rules has become the flexibility required for sensible policy-oriented decision making.... In other words, we justify as legal sophistication what the classics would have viewed as the obvious abandonment of legality' (1998: 36).

2 Equal Employment Opportunity Commission (1991), 'Guidelines on Discrimination Because of Sex', 29 C.F.R. Sec. 1604.

3 Unofficial translation. There is also a federal Equal Treatment Law that was passed, applying to federal workers, although they do not have an Equal Treatment lawyer and the remedies for violations of the statute are different from those under the private law.

4 The Equal Treatment Commission (GBK) has interpreted this as meaning that it is not the intention of the aggressor but rather the subjective impression of the complainant of having been harassed which determines whether sexual harassment has occurred. This is a similar standard to the US standard of reasonable woman/victim set forth in *Ellickson* v. *Brady* (1991). However, unlike US cases, decisions made by the GBK are not binding in Austrian courts.

5 In the USA, the Supreme Court looks at evidence relevant to the 'totality of circumstances' (*Vinson*, at 69) in determining welcomeness.

6 *Harris* v. *Forklift Systems, Inc*, 510 U.S. 17, 22 (1993) and *Vinson*.

7 *Harris*, at 22. Judges are directed to consider four factors: (1) the frequency and (2) severity of the conduct, (3) whether it is physically threatening or humiliating, or mere offensive utterances, and (4) whether it unreasonably interferes with an employee's work performance. (Psychological injury might be considered a fifth factor, but is not necessary to a claim of hostile environment sexual harassment.)

8 When considering a hostile environment case, behavior might not reach the threshold of impairing personal dignity, but could still be considered sexual harassment if it was frequent or continuous (Bei and Novak, 1997). The crucial aspect, however, 'is whether the work atmosphere has become unbearable for the victim' (ibid.: 127).

9 The *Vinson* decision further found that victims can claim injuries even when these are not tangible, such as psychological injuries. In *Harris*, the court held, in another unanimous ruling, that in a hostile environment claim of sexual harassment, the injuries need not 'seriously affect [the employee's] well-being or lead her to suffer injury' (ibid., at 302). Thus it was not necessary, according to the court, that the psychological injury of the victim be severe.

10 This enunciation of the standard for determining a hostile work environment came in the wake of a fierce academic debate over whether a 'reasonable woman' standard should be used in hostile environment cases where the victim was a woman. Legal commentators suggested this standard 'better reflects women's varied experiences and offers genuine protection of the law' (DeCosse, 1992: 285; Dolkart, 1994). One Circuit Court had used this standard (*Ellison* v. *Brady*, 924 F.2d 872 (9th Cir. 1991)) but Juliano and Schwab (2000) found in their empirical examination of federal sexual harassment cases between 1986 and 1996 that only 7 per cent of cases in 1995, and 6 per cent in 1994, used a reasonable woman standard. Most courts in their study used the reasonable person standard or did not specify a standard.

11 It is possible that, in a hostile environment case, behavior might not reach the threshold of impairing personal dignity, but could still be considered sexual harassment if it was frequent or continuous (Bei and Novak, 1997).

12 The Equal Treatment Commission (GBK) has interpreted the statute similarly, suggesting that it is not the intention of the aggressor, but rather the subjective impression of the

complainant of having been harassed, which determines whether sexual harassment has occurred. However, unlike US cases, decisions made by the GBK are not binding in Austrian courts. Austrian courts have not clarified this issue beyond the statute.

13 The Austrian Code of Conduct construes this broadly, suggesting that the conduct can be 'physical, gestural or verbal' (Bei and Novak, 1997). The actual behavior must be severe enough to also 'impair personal dignity' (a standard drawn from the EU recommendation) which would include physical conduct and grabbing, but not 'whistling or unwelcome invitations to coffee or dinner' (ibid.: 124). The US law has no 'dignity' requirement, but US courts similarly struggle with where to draw the line.

14 She was called 'augetakelte polyestertussi' (Wien, 15 October 1996, ASG 24 Cga 170/95k).

15 GBG sec. 2 Abs 1a(2). Also see Austrian Civil Code (Allgemeines Buergerliches Gesetzbuch, ABGB sec. 1157). sec. 2a(7).

16 GBG sec. 2(1a). An Austrian labor court case held an organization directly liable for the sexual harassment of their CEO (ASG Wien 25.2.1994, 25 Cga 461/93) and jointly liable for the sexual harassment by a manager (Wien 26.6.1996, ASG 19 Cga 182/94). Although the responsibility of the corporation for the sexual harassment of their executives is not specified in the law, leading personnel are considered a 'special danger' to employees as regards sexual harassment (Tinhofer, 1994).

17 Tinhofer (1994) argues that leading personnel are a 'special danger' to employees that should be considered in determining whether the employer breached their duty of care. The labor court has held an organization directly liable for the sexual harassment of their CEO (ASG Wien 25.2.1994, 25 Cga 461/93).

18 ASG 19 Cga 182/94 26 June 1996.

19 For example, the duty of care owed to the employee is still ambiguous in practice. In one Equal Treatment Commission (GBK) case where the offender was also the employer, the GBK considered this issue. They found that, where a complainant was harassed in the course of receiving a quasi-medical treatment from her employer, the employer was guilty of sexual harassment. This was so even though the employee had voluntarily submitted to the treatment, knowing it would involve physical contact, although the complainant was not informed of the precise nature of the 'treatment'. The GBK used the same standard that would apply to a physician–patient relationship. The commission found that 'special relationship' between the employer and employee was not sufficiently respected in this instance. The Equal Treatment Commission does not have any legal authority, but this decision reflects the legal ambiguity on this issue in practice.

20 In 1998, the Supreme Court held that, if the threats are not carried out, courts should use the same analysis as is used for a hostile environment claim: *Burlington Industries, Inc* v. *Kimberly Ellerth*, 1998 U.S. LEXIS 4217 (1998). In Austria, the same analysis considering the employer's breach of duty of care is used for either type of sexual harassment. It is not a requirement in either legal system that the victim prove the harasser specifically intended to sexually harass the victim. The victim must prove only that the harassment and consequences occurred.

21 This refers to supervisors 'with immediate or successively higher authority over the employee' (*Faragher* v. *City of Boca Raton* (1998)).

22 29 C.F.R. sec. 1604.

23 See, for example, 29 C.F.R. 1604.11(d) (1997): '(d) With respect to conduct between fellow employees, an employer is responsible for acts of sexual harassment in the workplace where the employer (or its agents or supervisory employees) knows or should have known of the conduct, unless it can show that it took immediate and appropriate corrective action.'

24 In *Faragher*, the Supreme Court explained their reasoning for including an affirmative defense for employers: 'It would... implement clear statutory policy and complement the Government's Title VII enforcement efforts to recognize the employer's affirmative obligation to prevent violations and give credit here to employers who make reasonable efforts to discharge their duty. Indeed, a theory of vicarious liability for misuse of supervisory power would be at odds with the statutory policy if it failed to provide employers with some such incentive.'

25 A sexual harassment policy and procedures to resolve sexual harassment disputes are the primary examples of this preventive and corrective action.

26 Attorney's fees and some other litigation costs were also sometimes awarded to prevailing plaintiffs (Haney, 1993).

27 Passage of the Civil Rights Act of 1991 looked unlikely until the Senate Judicial Confirmation hearings of the appointment of Justice Thomas to serve on the US Supreme Court gained publicity (Runkel, 1994). Anita Hill charged that she had been sexually harassed by Justice Thomas while he was her supervisor. While Thomas was eventually confirmed to the US Supreme Court, awareness of sexual harassment was raised to such an extent that few lawmakers wanted to appear unsupportive of women's civil rights (ibid.). Compounding the problems of the Republican lawmakers in opposing the bill, David Duke, a former Ku Klux Klan leader, was leading the Republican ticket in the race for the governorship of Louisana (ibid.). Spurred by these two events, and the support of moderate Republicans, a compromise was finally reached in the Act, and it was signed by then President George Bush.

28 This capping of damages for victims of sexual discrimination (and sexual harassment) is in contrast to claims under state tort law such as assault and battery or intentional infliction of emotional distress. In addition, in claims of racial discrimination or discrimination based on national origin, under 42 U.S.C. sec. 1981, which is not available to victims of sexual discrimination, compensatory and punitive damages are not capped.

29 GBG, BGBI Nr 108/1979, idF BGBI Nr 290/1985, 410/1990 and 833/1992 sec. 2a.(7).

30 ASG Wien 25.2.94, 25 Cga 461/93.

31 ASG Wien 25.2.94, 25 Cga 461/93 was argued by a prominent private labor lawyer, commissioned by the Chamber of Employees. AS5000 was awarded against the harasser for each instance of sexual harassment against the complainant (totaling AS15 000, which is approximately $1200) – the full amount requested.

32 As of early 2000, women claiming sexual harassment in the labor courts have lost one case (because of an expired statute of limitations) and one case because it was determined not to be sexual harassment, but, for the most part, the very few plaintiffs who turn to the labor courts have been successful (ASG Wien 24 Cga 170/95k 15.10.96). The first case (ASG Wien 25.2.94, 25 Cga 461/93) regarding sexual harassment was argued by a prominent private labor lawyer, who was commissioned by the Chamber of Employees. The plaintiff was awarded AS5000 for each instance of sexual harassment – the full amount requested (around $1200).

33 This may vary with state law.

34 This book focuses on sexual harassment in employment in the USA under Title VII and does not cover the specific instance of sexual harassment in education, which is also covered under Title IX of the Education Amendment Act of 1972. Various states have enacted human rights violation statutes similar to Title VII. Sexual harassment suits might also be brought under state tort law, contract law, worker's compensation or unemployment compensation statutes such as assault and battery, intrusion, negligent hiring and the intentional infliction of emotional distress. There is no common law tort specifically for sexual harassment. While some courts have held that worker's compensation is the exclusive

remedy under state law for these claims (which yield far lower monetary awards than tort claims, others have allowed them to proceed (Korn, 1993).

35 One legal scholar points out that to find that worker's compensation is the exclusive remedy for sexual harassment in the workplace implies, in conjunction with the policy justification for worker's compensation statutes, that sexual harassment is 'a risk inherent in the workplace' (Korn, 1993: 1386).

36 GBK sec. 4–5.

37 The appointments to the Commission are sensitive to gender. The chairman of the Commission is the Minister for Women's Affairs, or someone appointed on behalf of the minister. Further, each appointing organization should by statute name at least one woman, so the commission has as members at least 50 per cent women. (Gleichbehandlungsgesetz), BGBI Nr 108/1979, idF BGBI Nr 290/1985, 410/1990 and 833/1992 sec. 3(3); ibid., sec. 3(5a).

38 Ibid., sec. 6(1).

39 Ibid. Parties and witnesses may be invited to address the GBK. The Commission has found for the complainant by default where the respondent failed to accept the Commission's invitation to appear and produce a statement.

40 Ibid., sec. 5(1)(3).

41 Ibid., sec. 6(2).

42 Ibid., sec. 6(3).

43 Ibid.

44 One could also go straight to court, without ever going to the Commission. Alternatively, one could go both to court and to the Commission. In this instance, the court would stay the proceedings until the Commission had made a decision, although the court is under no obligation to follow the decision of the Commission.

45 The 'in' ending connotes the female sex in German. Her duties include appearing before the Commission with cases and conducting investigations on behalf of the commission (Bei and Novak, 1997). The equal treatment lawyer (and one lawyer serving as a vice-equal treatment lawyer) represent claims to the Commission throughout Austria.

46 GBG sec. 3a. The equal treatment lawyer is institutionally supported by the Department of Women's Affairs in the Federal Chancellory and appointed for an unspecified term.

47 The equal treatment lawyer is required by statute to hold office hours for consultation with individuals claiming violations of the GBG (Gleichbehandlungsgesetz), BGBI Nr 108/1979, idF BGBI Nr 290/1985, 410/1990 and 833/1992 sec. 3a(2).

48 Ibid., sec. 3a(3).

49 Upon submission, the Commission must begin procedures on the case during the next session, but, at the latest, within one month (ibid., sec. 3a(4)). The Commission must then either provide an opinion on the question of equal treatment under sec. 5, or must begin an investigation of a specific claim of equal treatment under sec. 6A of the Equal Treatment Act. Section 6A states that, if the equal treatment lawyer's interpretation of the case does not correspond to the decision of the GBK, the complainant can go to the labor court for recourse, where the decision of the GBK does not have precedential value.

50 Each state ('Land') within Austria has its own Chamber of Labor.

4 The Social Context of Sexual Harassment: Managerial Interpretations of the Law

Introduction

Managers at each of the five organizational case studies varied in their perceptions of the legal harm of sexual harassment. However, rather than expressing five different interpretations of sexual harassment, I found three distinct models or 'templates' for interpreting illegality. Rather than merely the result of national differences in law, these templates reflect the results of differences in social context, derived at both the national and organizational levels. I labeled these three different interpretations of sexual harassment the Legitimacy Challenge, Bureaucratic Compliance and Risk Management. Table 4.1 highlights the ways managers understood and implemented sexual harassment law in these firms.[1]

I conducted management interviews at five firms: Alpen, Hudson, Prairie, Jet Stream and Gulf Stream. Although this is developed in more detail below, managers at Alpen, the Austrian domestic firm, and Gulf Stream, a US multinational in Austria, employed the Legitimacy Challenge template. In doing so, they rejected the issue of sexual harassment as an Austrian problem. To the extent that the problem of sexual harassment is accepted, managers employing this template limited it to organizational contexts other than their own. The issue of sexual harassment is not construed as an organizational risk by managers adopting the Legitimacy Challenge template.

Managers at the second multinational in the study, Jet Stream, employed the Bureaucratic Compliance template. They did so by responding to law through organizational rules that are formalistic, but not used in practice. Further, they understood sexual harassment as a risk to the organization, but were not overwhelmed by this risk. Finally, managers at the two US domestic firms, Hudson and Prairie, employed the Risk Management template. In doing so, they construed sexual harassment as a financial risk and took various steps

Table 4.1: Variation in perceptions of law: managerial templates

Legitimacy Challenge Reject problem, non-indigenous If problem exists, regulate others Not an organizational risk
Bureaucratic Compliance Legal responses through organizational rules Formalistic, not used in practice Accept problem as an organizational risk
Risk Management Accept problem as a financial risk Reduce risk through: • defensive legal strategies • expansion of regulated conduct • misinterpreted law • reliance on organizational standards of conduct

to reduce it, such as defensive legal strategies and expansion of the range of internally regulated conduct.

I now turn to each of the firms in more detail.

Descriptions of the Firms

Alpen: Austrian Domestic Firm

Alpen, an Austrian domestic pharmaceutical firm, is located in Vienna. Distribution of pharmaceuticals is the main function of Alpen. About half of their employees are female; similarly an estimated 50 per cent of their managers are female. The employees at Alpen are almost exclusively Austrian and between 50 and 60 per cent of their employees belong to a union. Alpen's CEO describes their organizational culture as rule-attentive and hierarchical.

Hudson and Prairie: US Domestic Firms

Hudson and Prairie, the two US domestic firms, are located in different parts of the United States. Hudson is on the east coast, while Prairie is in the midwest. Neither firm is unionized. Hudson's main function is research and development.

Hudson's managers estimate that 47 per cent of their employees are female and 31per cent of their managers are female. Prairie's work is more diversified than Hudson's, including manufacturing as well as research and development. It is larger by six employees, and 42 per cent of Prairie's employees are women. Just one-fifth of its managers are female. Hudson's managers describe their organizational culture as close-knit employees, team-oriented and open. The organizational culture at Prairie is described by its managers as formal and direct. They are in the process of moving away from a too hierarchical culture, towards lower-level decision making.

Jet Stream and Gulf Stream: US Multinational Firms in Austria

Both multinationals participating in this study are headquartered in northeast USA and have a regional headquarters in Europe. At the time of the interviews, managers reported that there were no US citizens employed in their firms, nor were they unionized. Both companies employ Austrians almost exclusively, although the CEO of Jet Stream is from another Western European country. Jet Stream employs 60 per cent women and, by their own estimation, 40 per cent of their managers are female. Gulf Stream estimates that 13 per cent of its managers and 40 per cent of its employees are female. Jet Stream's organizational culture, as described by its CEO, is rule-attentive and team-oriented. They are also moving towards lower-level decision making. Gulf Stream's managers describe the firm's movement as shifting from a conservative culture to something more open. They also recently instituted a Total Quality Management Program.

A summary of the above firms is provided in Table 4.2.

Given these demographically similar firms, but placed in different national contexts and with different organizational cultures, managers were found to have different perceptions of sexual harassment law; their contextualization of sexual harassment was based on aspects of their social context. The social context that was relevant to their legal understandings included elements from both the national and the organizational contexts. Below, the three templates are reviewed as regards response to law, and the implications for each of these templates within the organization are then discussed.

Legitimacy Challenge

First, the Legitimacy Challenge template was used by two firms in Austria, the Austrian domestic firm, Alpen, and Gulf Stream, one of the US multinationals. Managers who adopt this template reject the problem of sexual harassment and the state's authority to regulate in the area of sexual harassment.

Table 4.2 Summary information about the firms

	US Domestic		US Multinationals in Austria		Austrian Domestic
	Hudson	Prairie	Jet Stream	Gulf Stream	Alpen
Female employees (%)	47	42	60	50	55
Female managers[1] (%)	31	20	45	12.5	50
Number of employees (mean of sample = 56 median = 56[2])	below mean	above mean	above mean	above mean	below mean
Nationality of employees	85–90% US citizens	97% US citizens	90% Austrian	100% Austrian	90% Austrian
Primary functions	research and development	research and development, production	marketing, sales, finance and distribution	marketing, sales, administration, medical support	distribution
Managers' description of organizational culture	Close-knit employees open, team-oriented	Formal and straightforward employees, moving toward lower-level decision making	Very attentive to rules, team-oriented, moving toward lower-level decision making	Recently instituted Total Quality Management Program Moving from conservative to more open	Very attentive to rules and procedures, hierarchical

Notes:
1 The status of 'manager' was determined by the organization's own classification scheme.
2 The specific numbers of employees is not disclosed because of confidentiality concerns.

They shift the context of sexual harassment from the legal sphere to the political sphere. For example, the CEO of Alpen describes sexual harassment as part of international politics:

> Sexual harassment is not an Austrian problem. It's an American problem imposed on Austria. The United States tells countries they should do something according to the law, but then does whatever they want – regardless of the law. (Alpen 1.1)

To managers employing the Legitimacy Challenge template, the technical demands of law are inseparable from its political implications.[2] For example,

Alpen's CEO drew on the values of Austrian cultural autonomy to reject the liberal legal assumption of law as distinct from politics and replace it with a critical assessment of the US export of legal concepts. Recasting it as an expression of American colonialism, this manager shifted discussions of sexual harassment law to predictable cultural battle lines of US imposition. What it is not, according to this view, is an issue relevant to Austrian people or to Austrian organizations.

Just as Alpen's CEO challenged the legitimacy and relevance of sexual harassment law, managers at Gulf Stream similarly adopted the Legitimacy Challenge template. Gulf Stream's managers, working at the Austrian site of a US multinational, describe sexual harassment law as non-indigenous to Austria, and irrelevant to Austrian society:

> I have to say it's not at all covered in our company policies because it is not really an issue in our thinking and behavior. It's not even mentioned. I think sexual harassment has never been an issue in Austria.

Although Gulf Stream's managers employed the Legitimacy Challenge template, none of the managers at Gulf Stream expressed a normative concern about the political threat of sexual harassment law to the extent that it was expressed at Alpen. (They are, after all, employed by a US multinational.) Sexual harassment law was rejected as non-indigenous, but it was not characterized as a direct product of American legal colonialism.

To the extent that managers employing the Legitimacy Challenge template do recognize sexual harassment, it is confined to settings other than their own. Although the law contemplates sexual harassment as a type of discrimination, it was understood by managers employing this template only narrowly. When managers using the Legitimacy Challenge template consider sexual harassment as a problem that might occur in Austria, they confine it conceptually to sex workers (for example, women whose work involves sexual appeal), even though neither Austrian nor US laws make such a distinction:[3]

> Sexual harassment is just not an issue for Austrians and it is not an issue for our work. It's not part of our business. My employees come here and they do their job. They don't dress seductively or wear heavy make-up and nail polish because *that's not part of their work.* (Alpen 1.1)

Similarly, Gulf Stream's CEO reiterated the lawlike argument used at Alpen, suggesting that sexual harassment law was not relevant to Gulf Stream's operations because sex was not part of their business. However, he said that he 'could imagine that in some institutions or professions where women are addressed as a sexual subject, like a waitress, sexual harassment might be an issue' (Gulf Stream 2.3).

The rejection of the issue of sexual harassment in firms adopting the Legitimacy Challenge template is unfettered by concerns about the organizational consequences of a sexual harassment lawsuit, either financial or in terms of employee morale. Managers employing this template did not express concern about the financial consequences of a sexual harassment complaint and they do not have internal legal responses to sexual harassment such as a sexual harassment policy or a specific claims procedure for sexual harassment complaints. Gulf Stream's managers describe their knowledge of sexual harassment, but in employing the Legitimacy Challenge template, they did not try to maintain control of the issue through the use of internal law.

> We had general discussions [about sexual harassment]... you know over lunchtime when you are eating together... I mean we were also joking and we said, well, we have to be careful.... It's not written down [in a policy] but I think most people know about it. (Gulf Stream 2.4)

Gulf Stream did not have a sexual harassment policy, nor did it have complaint procedures specific to sexual harassment. Disputes would be handled informally (if they occurred) and without any particular documentation. Gulf Stream's home office communicated other management policies to the site, but the adoption of a sexual harassment policy was not actively promoted by headquarters. Because Gulf Stream's CEO employed the Legitimacy Challenge template, the US sexual harassment policy was not adopted at his site.

This is not to say that managers employing the Legitimacy Challenge template are entirely unconcerned about sexual harassment complaints. While this issue was not addressed by Alpen's manager other than to indicate its absence, Gulf Stream's management spoke, not of the financial risk, but of the personal risk associated with sexual harassment:

> I think it is a sensitive issue because of the risk. It's always difficult but if there's a person who just claims that you have been doing something which you're not allowed to do, it can cause very big problems... You hear jokes on the radio, everywhere. But if it is addressed toward one person that she... perceives it sensitively, then this can be an issue... If somebody wants to cause you problems, then they could do it. (Gulf Stream 2.5)

Bureaucratic Compliance

Managers using the second template for interpreting illegality, Bureaucratic Compliance, accept sexual harassment as an organizational issue and respond to sexual harassment formally through rules that are, in practice, unused. For example, Jet Stream's management identified sexual harassment law as an issue of employee morale and, more importantly, an issue of potential financial liability. Unlike the other firms in Austria, Jet Stream's managers defined sexual harassment through a policy:

> We are used to abiding by the law. If there's a law on sexual harassment . . . we try to meet what thc law stipulates. Culturally, we think we are a US corporation. My experience in a US corporate setting is that one believes that everything can be dealt with by policies.

The policy-driven response of US firms was seen by the European (but non-Austrian) CEO in juxtaposition to the informality that dominates Austrian firms. However, the adoption of a formal policy on sexual harassment in the Bureaucratic Compliance template is more superficial than substantive. For example, according to Jet Stream's CEO, it had never been used at the site, and the policy itself is much less detailed than the policies at either of the US domestic firms – and is just one page long. Its definitions of sexual harassment very closely parallel the formal law, but it does not elaborate on any definitions or penalties.

Like a Weberian ideal type, this formalistic conception of law is not realized and routinized within organizational practice. The policy had never been used at the Austrian site. Jet Stream's CEO described how it is within managerial discretion to define the nature of employee disputes:

> We have rules and we have training. It really depends on how you look at it. It can be a dispute from an employee point of view and, from a management point of view, it is lack of performance. (Jet Stream 1.4)

Finally, for managers employing the Bureaucratic Compliance template, the issue of sexual harassment is one worthy of organizational concern. For example, managers at Jet Stream were attentive to sexual harassment law, because it was an issue of 'employee morale and job satisfaction' (Jet Stream 1.2), but, more importantly, because it was seen as a potential financial threat to the firm. This theme is one we will see again when considering the Risk Management template.

Risk Management

The third way managers interpreted illegality is through the Risk Management template. Managers using this template were concerned about financial liability and responded to law in ways that reduced the risk of sexual harassment liability. They did this by using defensive legal strategies and by expanding the range of internally regulated conduct.

Managers at the two US domestic firms, Hudson and Prairie, used the risk management template and reduced their perceived risk through formal responses. They adopted sexual harassment policies, they disseminated those policies to employees, they developed sexual harassment complaint procedures – they had all the responses a good lawyer would recommend. These managerial actions were clearly legal strategies introduced with the intent of reducing financial liability. As a manager at Prairie, tells it,

> All the attorneys will tell you, 'You need a sexual harassment policy.' We need to let people know what our policy is on sexual harassment – that it is something that won't be tolerated. But as the attorneys have told me, it's also a defense for the company should there be a charge of harassment. (Prairie 2.5)

Hudson's policy specifically set the standard for sexual harassment as welcomeness, stressing that it is up to the individual to decide if it is sexually harassing. The policy relies on a 'reasonable person of the same sex as the person harassed' to determine hostile environment sexual harassment.[4] In an easy-to-read style, the policy goes on to suggest that men and women may have different thresholds of offensiveness, so 'any improper conduct should be avoided'. Further, it includes a provision on fraternization and strongly discourages dating between individuals in different levels of the hierarchy. Even with the elaboration given in Hudson's policy, it is difficult to define specific instances that are or are not sexual harassment.

Prairie's sexual harassment policy was different in emphasis but similar in content, again closely linked to the EEOC guidelines. Prairie's policy reflected their organizational culture as it was described by managers: bureaucratic, conservative and hierarchical. Further, although Prairie had a human resource office that disseminated their sexual harassment policy, only 20 per cent of the employees responding to the survey at Prairie cited a managerial source of information about sexual harassment law. This is compared to 48 per cent at Hudson, where there was not a human resource office.[5]

The Prairie policy is two pages long, but defines the content of sexually harassing behavior in just one sentence. The rest of the policy is devoted to describing the investigation, (which culminates in a written report) and lays out the penalties for both alleged sexual harassment and 'proven' sexual harassment. Very legalistic in appearance, Prairie's policy does little to define the harm of sexual harassment, or to give standards for predicting whether something is or is not sexual harassment.

Even with their policy and other procedural defenses, managers employing the Risk Management template were pessimistic about the future. As Hudson's managers explain:

> We have all the policies in place, so no one can accuse us of not having a policy. Once you have a policy, as soon as an issue comes up, we address it immediately and pray like hell that common sense dictates. But I'm sure someday, somewhere, somehow, something will come up where common sense doesn't win out, and then we're all losers. (Hudson 18)

Managers employing the Risk Management template are particularly concerned about their vulnerability to false sexual harassment claims. For example, Hudson's managers recounted the actions of a female employee who had threatened a sexual discrimination lawsuit if she were not promoted, even though she had been working at the company only six months. The advice of their lawyers was to do nothing against the employee and take notes regarding the incident. Hudson's managers expressed frustration as they described the company's vulnerability to malicious lawsuits:

> Basically it's a no-lose situation for the person making the claim and it was a lose–lose situation for the company.... She essentially became immune to any action on our part because it would be viewed as a response to a claim. She basically did nothing for six months until she found another job... and she left. (Hudson 16)

The concern about false claims and the potential power of plaintiffs was inflamed by their lawyer's advice that there was nothing they could do without major financial risk. The combination of the perceived threat of undeserved lawsuits and the helplessness of the company in combating this type of sexual harassment suit led Hudson to a policy of 'zero tolerance'. The CEO describes the problem of running a business and having to be prepared for unjust claims:

> The practical issue for us is we've got a business to run. We've got to spend that time and our money and resources to run the business. We're not in the business of being vindictive. We're not in the business of being moralists. We're not in the business of telling people how to run their lives or what they should find offensive. The bottom line is that if you come here, you've got to enjoy work here.... The other side is, once lawyers are involved, once rules and regulations are twisted and played with – we're out of our league. This is not our business. We're not lawyers, harassment experts or discrimination experts. (Hudson 16–17)

The second way managers reduced risk using the Risk Management template was by enlarging the range of regulated conduct. Although none of the managers spoke specifically about awards in sexual harassment cases, they were convinced that employer liability would be very high. Law was (mis)understood by managers at both firms on this issue. While sexual harassment law is complicated (even to lawyers and judges), these managers understood the law in ways that increased its threat and, as will be discussed later, expanded its scope.[6] This was done through key misinterpretations of the law and through a shift from legal standards of conduct to organizational ones. First, managers assumed employer liability in all instances of sexual harassment. This is not an accurate portrayal of sexual harassment law. As described in Chapter 3, in this area, the US law is very complex. In fact, the Supreme Court was recently forced to rule in this area because of all of the different rules employed by various courts. Employer liability is very much dependent on the facts in each case.

The third way managers reduced risk was to rely only on the subjective standard for determining sexual harassment. This standard refers *only* to hostile environment cases and is used *only* in conjunction with a reasonableness standard. Hudson's managers describe their standard:

> It's the individual standard that the company chooses to recognize.... We try and set the standard to what each individual sees. If someone is uncomfortable with [behavior], it'll be addressed. It's the company's goal to address that. (Hudson 12–13)

This shift from the law – and their own written policy – enlarges the scope of sexual harassment law. Prairie, similarly, used the subjective standard in considering what sorts of behavior fall under the definition of sexual harassment, describing sexual harassment as 'in the eye of the beholder' (Prairie 2.12).[7]

Managers also expanded the *scope* of the law by relying on organizational standards of conduct rather than legal definitions, a far cry from the legal framework of discrimination based on sex.

> If you have a culture that encourages employee interaction but appropriate courtesies are to observed at all times, I think that really helps maintain it. We just hired good people here... they know if they have a behavior that doesn't fit in, we will go wherever we have to go to find their replacement and we'll find it.... But for the most part, I think people have understood about that sense of courtesy. (Hudson 19, 21)

In implementing sexual harassment law, managers employing the Risk Management template shift substance of the law from anti-discrimination to one of organizational context. Organizational norms regulate what might otherwise be regulated by sexual harassment law, although the regulation takes place under the guise – and the legitimacy – of sexual harassment law. The more accessible concepts of respect and sensitivity, readily available in the organizational context of the organizations, replaced the legal words found in Prairie's sexual harassment policy or in the law, and are used to evaluate sexual harassment claims:

> What is respect for people? It's what's right and what's wrong. . . . If it's not something you could say in front of your wife or your spouse and feel comfortable with it, then its probably not something you should say to somebody else. (Prairie 2.14)

> Sexual harassment is certainly an important issue, but it's a non-issue. It's not a problem, it's not something that happens here. It's not something that we dwell on. It just seems like its part of our values – respect for people – and I think that works for us. (Prairie 2.5)

Similarly, Hudson's employees are respectful of one other. Hudson's managers suggest the employees' sensitivity is derived from the particular culture of their organization:

> It's probably a mini-United Nations over here. We've got multiple languages, multiple backgrounds, older people, younger people, black, white, Hispanic, Indians, Chinese. Every one of the world's religions is represented here. It creates a sensitivity to people on how they interact with each other. . . . There's a level of caring. (Hudson 17–19)

Discussion

These findings suggest that, even when laws regulating illegality are similar, they are understood through their social context. Differences in the national contexts of the USA and Austria were found that are reflected in the differing perceptions of these managers, as described in the three templates. In the Austrian national context, the concept of sexual harassment is often intertwined with its perceived source. As will be recalled from Chapter 2, during the parliamentary debates on the Austrian sexual harassment law many opponents of the law characterized it as an example of American cultural and political dominance. The Senate judiciary hearings over Clarence Thomas's nomination to the Supreme Court received extensive press in Austria, as did the Clinton impeachment hearings. In both instances, Austrian media characterized the USA as Puritanical and oppressive.

The theme of American dominance in the world is one that strikes a nationalistic chord in Austrian culture. Austria was occupied by the Allies for ten years after the end of World War II and, unlike much of the rest of Europe, became an officially neutral country during the cold war. Austria finally voted to join the European Union in the mid-1990s, but it was not without concern for Austrian cultural and political independence.

This concern for Austrian cultural autonomy and the aspect of national context is clearly reflected in the Legitimacy Challenge template. What we do not see reflected by managers is that the Austrian law is stronger than EU law and the laws of many of her European neighbors because it casts sexual harassment as a discrimination and not merely an indignity. Further, Austrian law provides monetary awards for each instance of sexual harassment, even if the harm is not material. The political fight for a sexual harassment law between 1990 and 1992 was substantial. It received extensive press coverage as a problem of four out of five Austrian women (Hofpgartner and Zeichen, 1988). The push for the additions to the Austrian Equal Treatment Law, including sexual harassment, were so strong that labor unions threatened a strike if they were not passed.

The Austrian national context provides two competing accounts of sexual harassment, but only one was reflected in the perceptions of managers employing the Legitimacy Challenge template. By drawing on the issue of national autonomy, this template keeps sexual harassment in the political, rather than the legal, sphere, making estimations of illegality irrelevant as a matter of organizational life. The consequence for organizations that employ this template is the maintenance of the status quo. Sexual harassment claims are likely to be easily silenced once they are characterized as politically motivated or as un-Austrian.

The national context of the USA resulted in very different managerial interpretations of illegality. Sexual harassment, purely a domestic topic, is a financial issue to employers expressing the Risk Management template. We have all heard the litigation horror stories (Hayden, 1991) and these stories surrounding sexual harassment are alive and well in trade journals. For example, an insurance advertisement placed in several 1998 *Business Insurance* issues takes advantage of this fear of liability to sell insurance. The insurer offers up to $100 million in protection:

> So you still think an employment practices suit can't touch your company? In the past six years, the number of sexual harassment charges has doubled... And the revenues lost in courtroom battles have soared into the billions. The appropriate response: EPL Century Select. (*Business Insurance*, 21 December 1998, p.25)

Both by misinterpreting the law and by using diffuse organizational standards like respect and courtesy for others, managers using this template effectively expand what might be sexual harassment and increase their chances of successfully defending a lawsuit should one emerge. Just imagine, if the standard for sexual harassment is sensitivity to others, and it is up to any individual to define what that means: the range of potential illegality is huge.

But it could have been different had these managers drawn on other aspects of their national context. They could have drawn on the legal norms of group-based discrimination and contextualized sexual harassment as an issue of gender equality, or they could have rejected the law outright, and taken their chances. Sexual harassment was clearly established legally as a type of group-based sex discrimination by the mid-1980s, yet managers employing the Risk Management template cast their concern in terms of particular individuals (rather than groups) that might be a financial risk (not victims of discrimination) to the organization.

In fact, it is not that easy to bring a sexual harassment claim. Assuming one wants to litigate, which is a large assumption, it can be hard to find, much less pay, a lawyer. Over the ten years after *Meritor*, 54 per cent of plaintiffs in federal court won their cases against their employer (Juliano and Schwab, 2000), but they did not win much compared to other types of corporate lawsuits. Their average award was $80 000, according to Juliano and Schwab (1999) and earlier studies showed lower awards (see Terpstra and Baker, 1988).

The consequence of the Risk Management template is that sexual harassment law can be used as an aspect of organizational control. It can be a weapon for managers to get rid of male employees who are otherwise undesirable. It can also be used as a justification for excluding female workers from informal power networks because of male supervisors' concerns that they might be offended by informal banter, maintaining the barriers to women in the workplace.

While it is convenient to talk about national differences, I found that both the national and organizational contexts interact to create a much more complicated picture of the ways that social context filters interpretations of law. In each instance, these templates for interpreting illegality reflect norms that are consistent with *organizational purposes* as well as their national context. Most dramatically, the organizational context has a role in shifting attention from one national context to another.

Neither laws nor organizations are nationally bound and this matters for interpretations of sexual harassment law. Using the Bureaucratic Compliance template, Jet Stream, a US firm in Austria, with no US employees, talked the talk of a US firm, and indeed, believed they were one. They attended to US law and responded as they believed a US firm should – with a policy – even though they existed within the Austrian national context, and had never used the policy. Further, Jet Stream's management *chose* to respond to US law.

Given that the Austrian and US definitions of sexual harassment are similar, their choice was one of symbols rather than real difference. The responses to sexual harassment law may have been designed to appease their headquarters, but the consequences of the Bureaucratic Compliance template go deeper. Their employees operate under a different set of policies, rhetoric and rules than do the other Austrian employees in this study. In the next chapter, I will explore the role of both national and organizational context on employee understandings of sexual harassment law.

However, in the managerial interpretations of sexual harassment law, I find that interpretations of illegality are influenced by where one lives as well as where one works. In the face of many possible interpretations, organizational managers rely on those interpretations of illegality that are consistent with organizational purposes. This suggests that the success of current attempts to standardize new areas of commercial, criminal and human rights law will be interpreted through a social context that includes national, organizational and, as I will soon discuss, individual levels. The battle of legal standardization is not over with the passage of the legal text. We should expect that the defining issues of old battles won in the passing of laws will reappear when individuals give their own, contextual, interpretations of the law.

Notes

1 This concept of templates comes with a few caveats. First, the templates I have identified reflect these managerial perceptions of law, and do not comprise an exhaustive list. Second, these templates are not necessarily exclusive. While not the case in these examples, organizational decision makers may rely on more than one template in responding to law, or there may be other templates that are hybrids of the three I have identified.
2 The managerial perspective at Alpen is based on an interview with the CEO. These characterizations of sexual harassment law were supported by interviews with other Austrian industry representatives not included in this study.
3 There is a separate sexual harassment provision for federal workers in Austria.
4 This appears to be a hybrid of the reasonable woman standard used in the 9th Circuit.
5 The difference in information sources between employees at Hudson and Prairie is significant (chi square) at $p = 0.007$. Interestingly, employees at Prairie compared to Hudson employees were more likely to believe their firm was in compliance with sex discrimination law.
6 While I do not suggest that managers employing the Risk Management template intentionally misunderstand the law, in all of the interviews with managers employing this template it was never interpreted too narrowly.
7 Prairie's sexual harassment policy was silent on the issue of a subjective/objective standard in hostile environment cases.

5 The National, Organizational and Individual Levels of Social Context

Introduction

I now focus on the individual employee perceptions of law and consider the role of various aspects of social context. Because the focus in this book has been on a better understanding of the role of social context in the interpretation and implementation of law, I asked employees at four of the firms in this study to define sexual harassment law.[1] I explore individual understandings of law by presenting five sexual harassment vignettes, or fact patterns, to each employee which, among other things, examined when individuals will describe conduct as *illegal* sexual harassment. The survey explored individual understandings of the implementation of the law by asking these same individuals what they believe should be done by the organization in response to the conduct described in the vignettes.[2]

Employees rated the *legality* or *illegality* of the conduct described along an ordinal scale, from absolutely legal, probably legal, probably illegal to absolutely illegal. They were asked to do this with reference to the laws of the USA or Austria, according to their own location. After each vignette, the survey indicated the recipient of the conduct, the female 'victim', who complained to her company about the conduct of the male 'harasser' (although neither of these labels is ever used in the questionnaire). The employees were asked to evaluate potential responses by the company according to how strongly they agreed that the company should fire the 'harasser'.

Below are the texts of the vignettes contained in the survey (see Appendix II):

Seductive behavior: Ms. Ebner is the only female manager in her department at Firm X. Her supervisor, Mr. Frank, often talks about every detail of Ms. Ebner's physical appearance. For example Mr. Frank has asked Ms. Ebner what bra size she wears, and whether she wears underwear. Ms. Ebner has asked Mr Frank to stop this behavior.

Gender harassment: Ms. Abel is the only female manager in her department at firm X. Mr. Bauer, her supervisor, often tells Ms. Abel that she has no business being in the management department and that she belongs home in the kitchen. When Ms. Abel arrives at the office, her supervisor says, "Why do you bother coming to work? Only men belong here." Ms. Abel asked Mr. Bauer to stop making these statements.

Sexual imposition: Mr. Lang found his secretary, Ms. Meyer alone in the office. Although they did not have a sexual relationship with each other, he grabbed her breasts against her will.

Illegality

Using these vignettes to explore empirically what employees define as within or outside the law, as well as whether and how aspects of the social context are related to these understandings of law, I found that most individuals believed these vignettes were examples of illegal sexual harassment under the laws of their own nation. As seen in Table 5.1, approximately 85 per cent of employees believe that the gender harassment and seductive behavior vignettes are examples of sexually harassing conduct. When describing the sexual imposition vignette, employees almost unanimously identified the conduct as absolutely illegal. While it is interesting in itself that so many employees clearly understood this conduct to be illegal, this makes further quantitative explanatory analysis of the contributions of the various organizational and national aspects of social context impossible, since there is little variability to explain.

Table 5.1 Estimations of illegality

Illegality	Seductive Behavior	Gender Harassment	Sexual Imposition
Absolutely legal (1)	5% (6)	5% (7)	1% (1)
Probably legal (2)	9% (12)	10% (13)	1% (1)
Probably illegal (3)	22% (29)	18% (24)	7% (10)
Absolutely illegal (4)	64% (83)	66% (87)	91% (124)
Total	100% (n = 130)	100% (n = 131)	100% (n = 136)
	Mean: 3.45	Mean: 3.46	Mean: 3.89
	Std. dev.: .86	Std. dev.: .88	Std. dev.: .40

It is interesting that so many employees were willing to find the gender harassment (the 'go back to the kitchen' conduct) illegal, since, in the United States, few courts are willing to call this conduct alone sexual harassment (Juliano and Schwab, 2000; Schultz, 1998). In Austria, no sexual harassment cases have been brought with this type of fact pattern, but on the basis of legal trends, it is unlikely to be included within the 'sexual sphere'.[3]

In addition to finding the conduct illegal, a similar percentage of employees (65 per cent) identified that conduct as a type of sexual harassment. However, employees were more likely to identify the seductive behavior (96 per cent) and the sexual imposition (99 per cent) conduct as sexually harassing, suggesting that gender harassment is not as clearly within the domain of sexual harassment. What employees identify as sexual harassment and what they identify as absolutely illegal in the seductive behavior vignette is also interesting. It suggests that, except for the gender harassment vignette, employees view the law as narrowing the field of sexually harassing conduct. Employees are less likely to say conduct is illegal than they are to call it sexual harassment, especially in the seductive behavior vignette.

On the basis of these dependent variables of 'illegality', I quantitatively examined the role of organizational and national aspects of social context on individual estimations of illegality. My analysis focuses, not on the differences between the vignettes, as discussed above, but on what contributes to these estimations of illegality.

Support for Punitive Organizational Action

Believing conduct is illegal, and thinking something should be done about it, are, in reality, two different things. In the sexual harassment context, most punitive action takes place, not in the courts, but within organizations. I asked these employees whether they thought the protagonist or 'harasser' in the sexual harassment vignettes should be subject to some type of punitive organizational action, although I left it to the respondent to determine whether the conduct breaks a law. For ease of discussion, I refer to this individual as the 'harasser', although this label was not used in the actual survey.

In general, employees were most willing to support the most severe organizational actions in the sexual imposition vignette, where almost 90 per cent of employees supported either transfer or dismissal of the 'harasser'. In the seductive behavior and gender harassment vignettes, about two-thirds of employees supported transfer or dismissal of the harasser. Almost no employees suggested the employer do nothing against the harasser. Asking the harasser to receive psychological counseling was, likewise, unpopular. These general findings reflect strong support for punitive organizational action in each of these vignettes. To explore what contributes to support for punitive organizational action, I focus more fully on support for the *most severe* organizational action against the 'harassers', employee dismissal. More fully elaborated in Table 5.2, 'agree' reflects support for discharge, while 'disagree' means the harasser should not be dismissed by the employer.

Table 5.2 Employee support for dismissal of 'harasser'

	Seductive Behavior	Gender Harassment	Sexual Imposition
Strongly disagree	21% (30)	32% (46)	11% (16)
Disagree	16% (23)	37% (52)	19% (27)
Agree	37% (52)	16% (23)	22% (31)
Strongly agree	25% (37)	15% (21)	49% (70)
Total	100% (n = 142)	100% (n = 142)	100% (n = 144)

Over half of the employees agreed or strongly agreed that the harasser should be discharged. Chapter 6 explores more fully the role of social context and the national, organizational and individual levels in explaining support.

The Model: National Context and Organizational Context

The Role of National Context

I turn first to the national context to describe the role of social context on understandings of law and its implementation. Because law tends to be derived from legal jurisdictions based on the territory of the nation-state, the national context most obviously provides the formal law regulating the organization. Legal decisions, the type of legal system, legal norms and procedures are all part of the national context surrounding law. However, the information provided by the national context extends beyond purely technical legal information. Cultural beliefs about the purpose of the law, its history and social impact all provide a context for law. The national context is likely to include legal and/or social information derived from non-national sources, such as media reporting on law.[4]

Measurements of National Context

I measure national context in two ways. First, I created a 'nation' variable for the nation in which the employee works: either the USA or Austria. As may be recalled from Chapter 4, almost all employees in the US site firms are US citizens and almost all employees in the Austrian firms are Austrian citizens. As used in the model, as a proxy for national context, this variable does not reflect citizenship, but the national site. I secondly measured national context by whether or not the employee received information about sexual harassment law from a media source. Media reporting on sexual harassment will reflect some aspects of national context (see Table 5.3). To the extent that this influences employee understandings of illegality, it will be evident in these models. This variable does not reflect the actual content of the information, but whether or not the employee learned something about sexual harassment law from a media source. There is no significant difference in whether employees received information from a media source when comparing companies (see Table 5.3). However, employees in Austria were more likely to receive information about sexual harassment law from a news media source than were employees in the USA ($p = 0.029$).

Table 5.3 National context

	Prairie	Hudson	Jet Stream	Gulf Stream	Pr> Chi2
Nation	USA	USA	Austria	Austria	–
News media source	69%	70%	81%	71%	0.53

The Role of Organizational Context

The organizational context also contributes to perceptions about law. Organizations present norms of informal exchanges and disagreements and often provide rules regulating employees and internal disputes. Courts largely rely on organizations to implement sexual harassment law. For example, in the US, having a sexual harassment policy and dissemination of information about sexual harassment law are two aspects of the organizational context that also have specific legal implications. However, the role organizational context plays on individual understandings of law remains largely unexplored[5] and virtually ignored in the international context. The present study considers several aspects of the organizational context for their potential to influence the ways individuals understand and implement law.

Measurements of Organizational Context

The model on the following pages includes three variables based on the organizational context: whether or not the company has a sexual harassment policy (referred to as 'policy'), whether the employee received information about sexual harassment law from a company source, and whether the employee believes the conduct violates an organizational rule.

Three of the four organizations in this part of the study had a sexual harassment policy: the two US domestic firms, Hudson and Prairie, and Jet Stream, one of the US multinational firms in Austria.[6] In this analysis, only the US multinational Gulf Stream, whose managers employed a Legitimacy Challenge template, as described in Chapter 4, does not have a policy.

I also created a variable based on whether the employee learned something about sexual harassment law from a company source, such as a special training program, a personnel department or employee, a written policy or rule, or a manager (survey results are contained in Table 5.4). Employees at the two US domestic firms, Hudson and Prairie, were more likely to receive information about sexual harassment from their employer than were employees at the US firms in Austria, although employees at Jet Stream were more likely to receive company information than were employees at Gulf Stream (see Table 5.4). This may reflect the fact that Gulf Stream does not have a sexual harassment policy. Jet Stream and Prairie are the only two companies with an established human resources office whose tasks included sexual harassment issues. It is interesting that employees at Prairie and Hudson were equally likely to receive information from a company source, considering that Prairie had a human resources office and Hudson did not.

Table 5.4 Organizational context

	Prairie	Hudson	Jet Stream	Gulf Stream	Pr> Chi2
Received information about sexual harassment law: company source	81%	81%	36%	4%	0.00
Has sexual harassment policy	yes	yes	yes	no	–

I measure aspects of the organizational context quantitatively through employee perceptions of organizational rules, whether the company has a sexual harassment policy and whether the employee received information about sexual harassment law from a company source. Employees also evaluated the extent to which the vignette conduct violated organizational rules. These *perceptions* of the organizational rules similarly show that the employees at Gulf Stream (the one firm relying on a legitimacy challenge and without a sexual harassment policy) are the least likely to identify conduct as violating organizational rules. Tables 5.5 to 5.7 show the responses for each of the three vignettes, by company.[7]

First, employee responses to the seductive behavior vignette are displayed in Table 5.5. At Jet Stream, Hudson and Prairie, almost all of the employees viewed the conduct as a clear violation of organizational rules. The perceptions of organizational rules were less uniform at Gulf Stream than at the other firms.

Table 5.5 Perceptions of organizational rules: seductive behavior

	Jet Stream	Gulf Stream	Prairie	Hudson	Total
Absolutely allowed	–	–	–	–	
Probably allowed	2%	13%	3%	4%	4%
Probably forbidden	19%	38%	19%	15%	21%
Absolutely forbidden	79%	50%	78%	81%	74%
					100%

Pearson chi2(6) = 11.05 Pr = .087

Differences among employees responding to the gender harassment vignette (Table 5.6) were again based on organizational borders rather than national borders. This time, however, employees at Prairie and Gulf Stream were the least sure that the conduct violated organizational rules. This was also suggested by the qualitative research on the firms. Gulf Stream did not address sexual harassment in company policy.[8] Further, while Prairie had a sexual harassment policy and dissemination, Prairie's policy was much more legalistic and ambiguous than the policy used at Hudson. Hudson's policy, although also ambiguous, more clearly covered gender harassment and it was easier to understand. Dissemination of the sexual harassment policy at Hudson was also much more interactive between management and employees than at Prairie.

Table 5.7 displays employee perceptions of organizational rules considering the sexual imposition vignette. Almost everyone responding to the survey believed that this conduct, the most severe of all the vignettes, was absolutely forbidden by their employer.

Table 5.6 Perceptions of organizational rules: gender harassment

	Jet Stream	Gulf Stream	Prairie	Hudson	Total
Absolutely allowed	0	4%	3%	0	1%
Probably allowed	2%	4%	5%	0	3%
Probably forbidden	16%	48%	19%	13%	21%
Absolutely forbidden	82%	43%	73%	88%	74%
					100%

Pearson chi2(9) = 18.34 Pr = .031

Table 5.7 Perceptions of organizational rules: sexual imposition

	Jet Stream	Gulf Stream	Prairie	Hudson	Total
Absolutely allowed	0	0	0	0	0
Probably allowed	0	0	0	0	0
Probably forbidden	2%	13%	3%	4%	4%
Absolutely forbidden	98%	88%	97%	96%	96%
					100%

Pearson chi2(3) = 5.32 Pr = .150

In the following analyses, three variables – whether or not the company has a sexual harassment policy, whether employees received information about a company source and whether the employee believes the conduct is prohibited by an organizational rule – are used to assess the role the organizational context plays on employee understandings of sexual harassment law and support for punitive organizational action.

The Model: Individual Differences as Part of Social Context

In addition to exploring the role of national context and organizational context, I consider a third aspect of social context in the role of socio-demographic characteristics in the understanding and implementation of sexual harassment law. By far the most empirical research on sexual harassment focuses on the role of gender differences in understandings of sexual harassment. The findings considering sex differences in understandings of sexual harassment are threefold. First, when compared to men, women tend to label more behaviors as sexual harassment (for example, Collins and Blodgett, 1981; Gutek *et al.*, 1983; Kenig and Ryan, 1986; Reilly *et al.*, 1982; Terpstra and Baker, 1987; Pryor and Day, 1988; Hunter and McClelland, 1991; Frazier *et al.*, 1995). Secondly, women tend to be less tolerant than men of sexually harassing behavior (Deitz-Uhler and Murrell, 1992; Kenig and Ryan, 1986). Finally, women are more likely than men to experience sexual harassment (Gutek, 1992; Konrad and Gutek, 1986; Tangri *et al.*, 1982; but see Saperstein *et al.*, 1991, and Powell, 1983).

Yet even with the large number of studies finding sex differences in understandings of sexually harassing behavior, there is some question as to how strong these differences really are. Gutek and O'Connor (1995) suggest (see also Frazier *et al.*, 1995) that, overall, sex differences in sexual harassment studies are not very strong, especially when considered in relation to other variables. While Gutek and O'Connor believe the differences are valid, they argue that differences between men and women are strongest in ambiguous situations, and weakest in the most severe and benign cases.[9] Beyond sex, there are few sociodemographic variables consistently examined in sexual harassment research. Most notable is the role of traditional attitudes and perceptions of sexual harassment. Some studies suggest that individuals with more traditional beliefs are less likely to label behavior as sexual harassment (Jensen and Gutek, 1982; Malovich and Stake, 1990; Deitz-Uhler and Murrell, 1992).

Measuring Sociodemographic Characteristics in the Model

In addition to the role of national and organizational contexts, the study controls for sex (male or female) since this has been an important variable in sexual harassment scholarship. In the overall sample, 43 per cent of employees are male. The study also examines the role of opposition to sex discrimination law in contributing to the understanding and implementation of sexual harassment law. I included this ideological litmus-test as a measure of individual difference. This measure is particularly interesting because one way to oppose the legitimacy of a law is to refuse to see it in its application, for example to deny conduct is illegal and/or that anything should be done about it.

I measured employee opposition to sex discrimination law by asking respondents to rate their support for anti-discrimination law on a five-point scale.[10] Three prompts were used to assess support for anti-discrimination law: 'I agree with the laws to protect women against discrimination', 'Laws against discrimination seem silly to me' and 'Laws against sex discrimination are necessary in today's society'[11] (Cronbach's alpha = 0.70). The responses to these questions were scaled, resulting in one variable ranging from 0 to 15, although responses ranged from 3 to 14. *Higher* numbers reflect greater *opposition* to sex discrimination law. Most employees expressed high support for anti-discrimination law. This variable is not significantly related to organizational context or nationality. Analyses presented in the next chapter show the role of organizational context and national context taking into account the effect of support for sex discrimination law.

Notes

1 The fifth firm did not participate in the survey component of this study.
2 See Appendix II for the survey. (Note that the formatting of the survey has been changed for presentation in this book.)
3 See Wien 15 October 1996, ASG 24 Cga 170/95k.
4 This is particularly likely in instances where nations have adopted similar statutes or joined legal jurisdictions (such as the European Union), or in the case of multinational organizations.
5 One exception to this statement is the work of James Gruber. While his work is focused on the success of various types of organizational action rather than the role the organization plays on individual understandings, his work marks a positive trend in sexual harassment research. Gruber (1998) suggests a link between policies and sexual harassment. On the basis of telephone survey responses of almost 2000 Canadian women, he suggests that official policies, procedures and training ('proactive methods') were more effective in reducing the more serious types of sexual harassment than 'informational methods' such as pamphlets or posters regarding sexual harassment (Gruber, 1997; 1998).
6 The variable 'policy' is coded 1 if the firm has a policy and 0 if the firm does not.
7 These results are reported as percentages. There are slight errors due to rounding.
8 The US office of Gulf Stream does have a sexual harassment policy.
9 Other scholars highlight within-group differences. For example, Schneider (1982) examined differences among women, finding that lesbian working women were more likely than heterosexual working women to define behavior as sexual harassment.
10 Responses to the second question were re-coded so that the direction of the responses was consistent with the other questions.
11 'Equal treatment laws' is used instead of 'Laws against sex discrimination' on the Austrian questionnaire.

6 Employee Perceptions of Illegal Sexual Harassment and Employee Support for Punitive Organizational Action

The Analysis

I begin with employee understandings of illegality and then turn to employee support for punitive organizational action. I use the same methods and largely the same model in both analyses. The higher the rating on 'illegality' the more likely the employee believes the conduct is illegal.[1]

The dependent variable of illegality includes four categories ranging from absolutely legal to absolutely illegal. This necessitated an ordered logit analysis. Similarly, support for employee discharge is also on an ordered scale, from strongly disagree to strongly agree.[2] The higher number, the more likely the employee supports employee termination. An ordered logit is a type of logistic regression that retains the categorical nature of ordered data. The advantage in using this procedure over other types of regression analyses is that each of the categories of the dependent variable are treated as separate categories that are ordered, rather than as a continuous variable. The regression equations provide the long odds that an increase in the independent variables will cause an increase in the level of the dependent variable (for example, from absolutely legal to probably legal, or from probably legal to probably illegal).

My presentation of the results focus on two primary aspects. First, I discuss the significance of the relationship between two variables. This means, taking into account the effects of the other variables in the model, how likely it is that these two variables are *actually* related and it does not just appear that way as a matter of chance. Standard social science practice is to consider findings of

0.05 and below a statistically significant finding (meaning five of every 100 relationships will be due to chance). On the tables to follow, I signify statistical significance with an asterisk.[3]

Second, I focus my discussion on the direction and strength of the relationship as reflected in the coefficient. In considering direction of the coefficient, a *positive* coefficient means that the variable is associated with a belief that the conduct is illegal, or support for termination. A *negative* coefficient means that variable is associated with a belief that the conduct is legal, and opposition to employee dismissal.

I now turn to the results of these analyses.

This chapter presents the findings on the role of social context and the importance of three distinct aspects of social context: organizational context, national context and individual difference. These results reflect the responses of employees in four organizational case studies.[4] I measured organizational context by whether the firm had a sexual harassment policy, whether the employee received information about sexual harassment law from a company source and whether the employee believed the conduct violated organizational rules. I measured national context by the national site of the employees' workplace and whether the employee received information from a media source. Finally, I include two sociodemographic characteristics, reflective of individual differences, with the focus on the role of sex, male or female, and opposition to sex discrimination law. The relationships among the variables measuring organizational context, national context and sociodemographic characteristics are reported taking into account the effects of other variables.

Influences on Perceptions of Illegality

I begin with employee understandings of the legality of the conduct expressed in the seductive behavior and gender harassment vignettes. Because almost all employees believed the sexual imposition vignette to be an example of illegal conduct (see previous chapter), there is little variation to explain through further statistical procedures. I first consider employee evaluations of the seductive behavior conduct. As discussed in the last chapter, most employees found this vignette to be probably (22 per cent) or absolutely (64 per cent) illegal conduct. Recall the vignette:

> *Seductive behavior*: Ms. Ebner is the only female manager in her department at Firm X. Her supervisor, Mr. Frank, often talks about every detail of Ms. Ebner's physical appearance. For example Mr. Frank has asked Ms. Ebner what bra size she wears, and whether she wears underwear. Ms. Ebner has asked Mr. Frank to stop this behavior.

My findings suggest that both organizational context and national context play a distinct part in individual employee understandings of law. Of the three organizational context variables, whether the company had a sexual harassment policy, whether the employee received information from a company source and whether the employee believes the conduct violates organizational rules, two were significant at the .05 level or below. If a firm had a sexual harassment policy, employees were significantly *less* likely to identify the seductive behavior vignette as illegal conduct (p = .03). There was an even stronger relationship between perceptions of organizational rules and estimations of illegality. Taking into account the effects of the other variables, the more employees identified the conduct as violating organizational rules, the more likely they were to also believe it was illegal, under their own national law (p = .00). Whether employees received sexual harassment information from a company source was not a statistically significant factor in employee understandings of illegality.

Turning to the national context variables, the national site and whether the employee received information about sexual harassment law from a media site, only national site obtained statistical significance below the .05 level, but the media source obtained borderline significance. Employees working in the United States were significantly more likely to identify the conduct as illegal than were employees working in Austria (p = .000). If the employee received information from a media source, they were slightly more likely to identify the conduct as illegal (p = .079).

Finally, taking into account the effects of the other variables, whether the employee was male or female did not significantly explain whether the employee found the conduct illegal. However, ideological opposition to sex discrimination laws was strongly related to understandings of illegality (p = .00). The more an employee opposed sex discrimination law, the less likely they were to identify the seductive behavior conduct as illegal (see Table 6.1).

The trends of employee responses to the gender harassment vignette are similar to those described above in the seductive behavior vignette, although fewer variables reached the level of statistical significance. Recall the vignette:

> *Gender harassment*: Ms. Abel is the only female manager in her department at firm X. Mr. Bauer, her supervisor, often tells Ms. Abel that she has no business being in the management department and that she belongs home in the kitchen. When Ms. Abel arrives at the office, her supervisor says, "Why do you bother coming to work? Only men belong here." Ms. Abel has asked Mr. Bauer to stop making these statements.

Again, a powerful role for the perceptions of organizational rules was observed. When an employee believed the gender harassment conduct to violate organizational rules, he or she was more likely to also believe it was illegal

Table 6.1 Labeling conduct illegal: seductive behavior vignette

Ordered logit estimates					n = 123	
					chi2(6) = 37.40	
					Prob > chi2 = .000	
Log likelihood = –100.28					Pseudo R2 = .1572	
Illegality	Coef.	Std. err.	Z	P>|z|	95% Conf. interval	
S.H. policy**	–1.38	.64	–2.16	.031	–2.3	–.12
Company source	.34	.47	.72	.473	–.58	1.26
Percept. org'l rule***	1.34	.35	3.82	.000	.65	–.05
Media source*	.83	.47	1.76	.079	–.10	2.02
Nation***	1.47	.52	2.83	.005	.45	2.49
Opposition to sex discr. law***	–.30	.08	–3.69	.000	–.47	–.14
Sex	–.27	.43	–.63	.530	–1.1	.57
Cut 1		–.52	1.24			
Cut 2		1.05	1.20			
Cut 3		2.85	1.25			

Notes:
Sexual harassment policy: categorical; 1 = company has sexual harassment policy.
Company source: categorical; 1 = received information about sexual harassment from company source.
Perception of organizational rule: ordinal; the higher the number the more the respondent believes the conduct is prohibited by company rules.
Media source: categorical; 1 = learned something about sexual harassment law from a media source.
Opposition to sex discrimination law: ordinal; higher numbers mean higher opposition to sex discrimination law.
Nation: categorical; 1 = US organizational site; 0 = Austrian organizational site.
Sex: categorical; 0 = female; 1 = male.

under their nation's laws (p = .00) (see Table 6.2). Further, as in the previous vignette (as can be seen in Table 6.2), if the firm had a sexual harassment policy, employees were *less* likely to find the conduct illegal. Unlike the outcome in the previous model, this relationship did not reach statistical significance. Again, whether the employee received information from a company source had no significant effect on their understanding of illegality.

On examining the role of the national context, taking into account the effects of the other variables, US employees were more likely to identify this conduct as illegal than were Austrian employees (p = .01). Further, if the employees received information about sexual harassment law from a media source, they were slightly more likely to find the conduct illegal, but this did not reach a statistical level of significance. A similar trend was observed for the socio-demographic variable, opposition to sex discrimination law. The more an employee opposed sex discrimination law, the less likely they were to identify conduct as illegal. This relationship did not reach statistical significance (p = .11). Despite the focus of sexual harassment researchers, the sex of the employee was not significantly related to understandings of illegality.

Table 6.2 Labeling conduct illegal: gender harassment vignette

Ordered logit estimates					n = 120 chi2(7) = 27.13 Prob > chi2 = .0003	
Log likelihood = −100.48					Pseudo R2 = .1189	
Illegality	Coef.	Std. err.	Z	P>|z|	95% Conf. interval	
S.H. policy	−.77	.61	−1.3	.206	−1.96	.42
Company source	−.01	.51	−.01	.991	−1.00	.99
Percept. org'l rule***	1.22	.34	3.61	.000	.56	1.88
Media source	.58	.50	1.18	.239	−.39	1.55
Nation***	1.38	.54	2.58	.010	.33	2.44
Opposition to sex discrim. law***	−.14	.09	−1.60	.110	−.30	.03
Sex	−.33	.44	−.76	.449	−1.20	.53
Cut 1		.50	1.31			
Cut 2		1.93	1.30			
Cut 3		3.18	1.34			

Notes:
Sexual harassment policy: categorical; 1 = company has sexual harassment policy.
Company source: categorical; 1 = received information about sexual harassment from company source.
Perception of organizational rule: ordinal; the higher the number the more the respondent believes the conduct is prohibited by company rules.
Media source: categorical; 1 = learned something about sexual harassment law from a media source.
Opposition to sex discrimination law: ordinal; higher numbers mean higher opposition to sex discrimination law.
Nation: categorical; 1 = US organizational site; 0 = Austrian organizational site.
Sex: categorical; 0 = female; 1 = male.

Employee Support for Punitive Organizational Action

I now turn to the issue of whether employees will support the dismissal of the protagonist in situations surrounding sexual harassment. That is, did they think the organizations should do something about the conduct? Dismissal in response to sexual harassment is the most serious of all employer responses and employers rely on employees to legitimize taking punitive measures. In this section, I explore the role of national context and organizational context, as well as individual sociodemographic factors, in whether or not employees will support employment action. Recall, from Table 5.2, that employee support for discharge varied greatly, depending on the nature of the conduct. Unlike estimations of illegality, there is sufficient variation in the sexual imposition vignette to include it in these analyses. While 49 per cent of employees strongly agreed with discharge in the sexual imposition vignette, only 15 per cent of employees strongly agreed with discharge on the gender harassment vignette. When considering seductive behavior, 25 per cent of employees supported termination. Beyond the particular context, I explore in the next section what it is that influences this support or lack thereof.

As in examining understandings of illegality, three variables are used to measure empirically organizational context: whether the company has a sexual harassment policy, whether the employee receives information from a company source and whether the employee believes the conduct violates an organizational rule. Likewise, two sociodemographic variables are included: the sex of the employee and opposition to sex discrimination laws. For national context, I continue to use the variables of national site and whether the employee received information from a media source, but an additional variable is included: estimations of illegality – whether the employee believes the conduct is illegal according to the laws of their nation – are used in this model as a reflection of national context, while in the previous section they were used as a dependent variable. If the illegality of the conduct under national law influences employee support for dismissal of the 'harasser', it will be revealed in this variable.

I begin with employee support for dismissal of the 'harasser' in the seductive behavior vignette. As displayed in Table 6.3, it was found that only one variable from organizational context, perceptions of organizational rules, is significantly related to support for termination ($p = .018$). Strikingly, *none* of the variables measuring national context is significantly related to support for termination. There were no significant differences based on national site, whether they received information from a media source or whether they thought the conduct was illegal. That is, taking into account the effects of the other variables, there was no difference based on whether the employee was American or Austrian, no difference based on whether they received information from a media source and no difference based on what they thought the law was. Again, sex did not significantly influence the result, but opposition to sex discrimination law did. Employees who were opposed to sex discrimination law were less likely to support termination (p = .05).

Table 6.3 Support for punitive organizational action: seductive behavior

Ordered logit estimates					n = 119 chi2(7) = 20.37 Prob > chi2 = .0090	
Log likelihood = −146.68					Pseudo R2 = .0649	
Illegality	Coef.	Std. err.	Z	P>|z|	95% Conf. interval	
S.H. policy	.04	.54	.07	.948	−1.01	1.08
Company source	.07	.41	.18	.861	−.72	.87
Percept. org'l rule**	.83	.35	2.37	.018	.142	1.52
Local law	.35	.25	1.39	.164	−.14	.83
Media source	−.48	.40	−1.21	.226	−1.26	2.30
Nation**	.22	.44	.50	.615	−.64	1.08
Opposition to sex discr. law**	−.17	.08	−1.99	.047	−.33	−.00
Sex	.08	.36	.23	.817	−.63	.80
Cut 1		2.09	1.40			
Cut 2		4.03	1.44			
Cut 3		4.82	1.46			

Notes:
Sexual harassment policy: categorical; 1 = company has sexual harassment policy.
Company source: categorical; 1 = received information about sexual harassment from company source.
Perception of organizational rule: ordinal; the higher the number the more the respondent believes the conduct is prohibited by company rules.
Perception of illegality: ordinal; the higher the number the more the respondent believes the conduct is illegal under national law.
Media source: categorical; 1 = learned something about sexual harassment law from a media source.
Opposition to sex discrimination law: ordinal; higher numbers mean higher opposition to sex discrimination law.
Nation: categorical; 1 = US organizational site; 0 = Austrian organizational site.
Sex: categorical; 0 = female; 1 = male.

Turning to the results of the gender harassment vignette, I find a similar importance of perceptions of organizational rules, taking into account the effects of the other variables (see Table 6.4). As displayed in Table 6.4, the more an employee believed the gender harassment vignette violated organizational rules, the more likely they supported dismissal ($p = .04$). Neither of the other organizational context variables reached statistical significance. Turning to national context, remarkably, I again found no difference in the responses of US and Austrian employees, taking into account the effects of the other variables. However, if an employee received information about sexual harassment law from a media source, they were significantly *less* likely to support dismissal. While not significant in the seductive behavior vignette described above, a similar trend was observed there. Again, whether the employee believed the conduct to violate national laws did not significantly influence employee support for dismissal. Finally, as is consistent with the seductive behavior vignette, employee opposition to sex discrimination law was significantly related to support for dismissal: if an employee opposed sex discrimination law, they were more likely to oppose termination ($p = .08$).

Finally, I consider the sexual imposition vignette. As displayed in Table 6.5, almost three-quarters of employees supported dismissal of the 'harasser' in response to this vignette. Unlike the previous models, these findings do not show a role for employee perceptions of the organizational rule. This is likely a statistical result of the unanimity of agreement that the conduct violated an organizational rule (100 per cent of respondents believed this was so). Considering the national context, only whether the employee had received information from a media source reached a level of statistical significance ($p = .04$). As in the other vignettes, if an employee received information from a media source, they were less likely to support dismissal. Finally, taking into account the effects of the other variables in the model, opposition to sex discrimination laws did not have a significant effect on employee support for dismissal.

Discussion

There were differences in the ways individuals understood sexual harassment law and these differences were the result of three distinct aspects of social context. Of the three aspects of social context, organizational, national and individual (as expressed through sociodemographic characteristics), there was support for each in contributing to whether employees label conduct illegal. First, there are national differences beyond those explained by the organizational context and by sociodemographic characteristics. Employees in the USA were more likely to find the conduct displayed in the vignettes

Table 6.4 Support for punitive organizational action: gender harassment

Ordered logit estimates					n = 116	
					chi2(7) = 18.80	
					Prob > chi2 = .0160	
Log likelihood = –142.70					Pseudo R2 = .0618	
Illegality	Coef.	Std. err.	Z	P>|z|	95% Conf. interval	
S.H. policy	.49	.55	.88	.381	–.60	1.57
Company source	–.26	.41	–.63	.528	–1.07	.55
Percept. org'l rule**	.69	.34	2.06	.039	.03	1.35
Local law	.01	.22	.04	.971	–.43	.44
Media source***	–1.14	.42	–2.71	.007	–1.97	–.32
Nation	.20	.46	.43	.665	–.70	1.09
Opposition to sex discr. law*	–.13	.08	–1.71	.087	–.28	.02
Sex	.17	.37	.45	.656	–.56	.89
Cut 1		.66	1.31			
Cut 2		2.40	1.33			
Cut 3		3.46	1.34			

Notes:
Sexual harassment policy: categorical; 1 = company has sexual harassment policy.
Company source: categorical; 1 = received information about sexual harassment from company source.
Perception of organizational rule: ordinal; the higher the number the more the respondent believes the conduct is prohibited by company rules.
Perception of illegality: ordinal; the higher the number the more the respondent believes the conduct is illegal under national law.
Media source: categorical; 1 = learned something about sexual harassment law from a media source.
Opposition to sex discrimination law: ordinal; higher numbers mean higher opposition to sex discrimination law.
Nation: categorical; 1 = US organizational site; 0 = Austrian organizational site.
Sex: categorical; 0 = female; 1 = male.

examples of *illegal* behavior. It was also found that, when employees received information on sexual harassment from the media, they were more likely to identify the conduct as illegal even taking into account the effect of national site. National context influences what conduct is perceived as illegal, even when laws define illegal conduct similarly.

Table 6.5 Support for punitive organizational action: sexual imposition

Ordered logit estimates					n = 127	
					chi2(7) = 8.62	
					Prob > chi2 = .3758	
Log likelihood = −153.46					Pseudo R2 = .0273	
Illegality	Coef.	Std. err.	Z	P>|z|	95% Conf. interval	
S.H. policy	.87	.53	1.63	.103	−.18	1.91
Company source	−.29	.40	−.73	.463	−1.07	.49
Percept. org'l rule	.00	.85	.00	.997	−1.67	1.68
Local law	.86	.59	1.46	.144	−.29	2.00
Media source**	−.87	.42	−2.10	.036	−1.69	−.06
Nation	−.32	.42	−.76	.447	−1.15	.51
Opposition to sex discr. law	.03	.08	.44	.663	−.12	.19
Sex	.34	.36	.93	.352	−.37	1.05
Cut 1		1.38	3.91			
Cut 2		2.65	3.91			
Cut 3		3.52	3.91			

Notes:
Sexual harassment policy: categorical; 1 = company has sexual harassment policy.
Company source: categorical; 1 = received information about sexual harassment from company source.
Perception of organizational rule: ordinal; the higher the number the more the respondent believes the conduct is prohibited by company rules.
Perception of illegality: ordinal; the higher the number the more the respondent believes the conduct is illegal under national law.
Media source: categorical; 1 = learned something about sexual harassment law from a media source.
Opposition to sex discrimination law: ordinal; higher numbers mean higher opposition to sex discrimination law.
Nation: categorical; 1 = US organizational site; 0 = Austrian organizational site.
Sex: categorical; 0 = female; 1 = male.

However, when I considered employee support for punitive organizational action against the 'harasser', I found that, of the national context variables, only a media source significantly influenced employee support. If an employee learned something about sexual harassment law from a media source, he or she was more likely not to support punitive organizational action. Recall that employees with a media source were also more likely to identify conduct as illegal. Thus employees receiving information from a media source are more likely to enlarge the range of conduct included under the law and less likely to support punitive measures as a result of the conduct. While my analysis does not examine the content of the information, only that it was received by the employee, it is likely that media reporting on sexual harassment delegitimates sexual harassment law by exaggerating the extent of the law, as well as the punitive results. This is an important area for future research.

It is striking that, net the effects of organizational context and sociodemographic characteristics, national site and estimations of illegality did not significantly explain support for organizational action. While Austrians were more likely to find conduct illegal, there was no national difference in support for organizational action. This is likely because, in considering internal action, employees focus on the internal context of the firm. Similarly, the illegality of the conduct under national law likely had no effect because employees viewed it as irrelevant to an internal punishment. Also recall that the firms in Austria were US multinational firms. This suggests that differences in perceptions of law may erroneously be attributed to differences in national context, when it may actually be the *organizational* context generating the interpretation. Having noted these mixed findings on the role of national context, I now turn to the role of sociodemographic characteristics.

First, ideological opposition to sex discrimination law in general influenced whether employees would identify particular conduct as illegal. This suggests that resistance to state regulation takes not just normative forms, but cognitive forms as well. Employees who disagree with sex discrimination law are less likely to use an illegal sexual harassment label to describe particular conduct. This was strongest in the seductive behavior vignette, which involved sexually suggestive comments without physical imposition. Ideological opposition to sex discrimination law also proved to be a significant factor in support for punitive organizational action. As one might expect, the greater opposition to sex discrimination law, the less likely one is to support the dismissal of the 'harasser'.

It is especially interesting that ideological opposition to sex discrimination law was so important, taking into account the effect of the other variables in the model. One might have expected national context to explain *all* of the differences in employee understandings of law, but this was not the case. This form of ideological resistance to law is particularly important within the context of sexual harassment law, and indeed much of employment law. If one were ideologically opposed to laws prohibiting murder, for example, it would make little difference in the implementation of laws against murder. While there might be some resistance in reporting murder, the implementation of law is largely done by the police and the formal legal system. However, the illegality of sexual harassment is largely assessed *within corporations*. Sexual harassment law is only in the rarest of circumstances implemented by the legal system, and legal trends in both the USA and Austria further define the use of the legal system as a last resort for these cases.

The implication of this finding is that ideological opposition to sex discrimination law among employees means that victims of sexual harassment are unlikely to gain legitimacy for their claims by stating that the conduct they experienced is illegal under national law. Employers are also unlikely to obtain support for internal organizational action against harassers if the organizational culture is one with strong ideological opposition to sex discrimination laws.

It is also interesting that the second sociodemographic variable, sex, had no significant effect in the model. Contrary to much of the earlier empirical work on sexual harassment, taking into account the effect of the other variables, women were not more likely to define conduct as illegal sexual harassment. However, empirical studies of sexual harassment largely fail to include the role of national context, ideological opposition to sex discrimination law and organizational context. While there are exceptions to each of these, no studies on understandings of sexual harassment have included each of these factors, together with the demographic characteristic of sex. The absence of these measures may explain earlier findings. This said, I do not suggest that sex has no influence on undertandings of illegality, only that it is not observed in difference in definitions of illegal conduct.

These results also make it clear that the organization is not just the site of sexual harassment in the workplace, but an interpretive context of sexual harassment law as well. Where one works fundamentally influences ideas about what sorts of conduct are illegal. First, taking into account the effect of national context, gender and ideological opposition to sex discrimination law, when an individual believes that the conduct is forbidden by *organizational rules*, he or she is significantly more likely to consider the conduct illegal under *national* law as well.[5] This finding shows a direct link between understandings of internal law and understandings of national law. Rather than relying solely on aspects of national culture to help decide whether something violates law, employees also rely on what they believe their organization prohibits. There is more to the interpretation of law than the national context.[6]

The role of organizational context was also marked by the finding that, when a firm adopted a sexual harassment policy, employees were *less* likely to believe the conduct was illegal under national law. This finding was strongest in the seductive behavior vignette (most clearly falling under the policies), but the trend was also observed in the gender harassment vignette. This shows another link between the organizational context and the external legal system: taking into account the effects of sociodemographic differences and national context, employees in firms with sexual harassment policies were less likely to believe that the conduct was an issue of *law*.

The promulgation of internal law, in the form of a sexual harassment policy, for instance, may make national law appear inapplicable. Firms with sexual harassment policies construe sexual harassment as a problem of *organizational* concern, and thus it appears less like a problem of national law, or illegality, and more an issue of organizational rules. Indeed, each of the firms with a sexual harassment policy (Hudson, Prairie and Jet Stream) did treat the problem of sexual harassment as an organizational problem, although they did this to differing degrees (see Chapter 4). It appears that, without the organization to 'solve' the sexual harassment problem, employees at the firm without a sexual harassment policy were more willing to define it under national law as illegal conduct, even taking into account the effect of national context and sociodemographic variables.

What makes this finding even more fascinating is that, like national law, these sexual harassment policies do little to spell out exactly what conduct is covered. They are ambiguous. It was not that the policies were far more specific than national law or more clearly spelled out the exact situations that are considered to violate organizational policy. Instead, the mere existence of a policy has the effect of making employees less likely to identify conduct as illegal under national law. Actual dissemination of information about the policy, or about sexual harassment law, in fact had *no significant effect* on whether employees would define the conduct as illegal. This finding is in direct conflict with the assumptions made in recent US Supreme Court decisions and EEOC policy about dissemination of sexual harassment information. Rather than having an actual effect on educating employees about illegal conduct, dissemination of information to employees is primarily a symbolic act that fulfills a legal notice requirement.

Remarkably, whether the firm has a sexual harassment policy and whether employees received information from a company source – two aspects of the organizational context that are also legally important in the USA – had no significant effect on whether employees would support punitive organizational action. Rather, it was whether the conduct was perceived to violate organizational rules that had the most significant relationship. Again, this suggests that the adoption of a policy, or even dissemination of information, has little real value to employees in their beliefs about what conduct should be punished. Instead, something more like due process standard appears to be at work. If employees believe the 'harasser' violated an organizational rule, they will be more likely to support punishment. Companies with sexual harassment policies will likely have employees who recognize that sexual harassment violates an organizational rule, but a sexual harassment policy and even its dissemination is not as important in explaining employee support for organizational action as what employees *actually think* the rules are.

Taken together, these findings detail the relative contributions of various factors in the social construction of sexual harassment law by individuals. Three aspects of the social context, individual, organizational and national, contributed to differing perceptions of law. Although sociodemographic differences receive much attention in studies of law (for example, Ehrenreich, 1991; Crenshaw, 1992) and in studies of sexual harassment (Gutek *et al.*, 1983; Kenig and Ryan, 1986; Reilly *et al.*, 1984; Terpstra and Baker, 1987; Pryor and Day, 1988; Baker *et al.*, 1990; Frazier *et al.*, 1995) there were few effects based on gender. In this study, the primary sociodemographic characteristic influenced understandings of illegality and support for punitive organizational action. Individual attitudes about law in general, such as ideological opposition to sex discrimination law, are clearly understudied. Attitudes about sex discrimination law influenced not just whether individuals will support internal punishment, but whether individuals believe a law has been violated at all.[7]

There was also a strong role for the national context in the application of law. This is expected because of the slight differences in law, but, more fundamentally, the larger differences in legal history, legal systems, procedures and legal culture. However, there was surprisingly little role for national site in support for punitive organizational action. National differences in law or culture did not explain support for internal organizational action.

Characteristics of the organization, generally ignored in cross-national studies and in all but the most recent sexual harassment studies, are important factors in contributing to the substantive understandings of law. Perceptions of what employers do in response to law influences whether or not individuals will perceive conduct as violating the law. It is clear that the organization is not just the site of sexual harassment in the workplace, but the social context of sexual harassment as well. Where you work, where you live, as well as who you are influences your ideas about what sorts of conduct are illegal and what should be done about them.

Notes

1 Because of the low variability on the sexual imposition vignette, I center my analysis on the gender harassment and seductive behavior vignettes. The mean of the sexual imposition vignette is statistically significantly different when compared to either the gender harassment or the seductive behavior vignette ($p = .00$; $p = 00$) in a paired t-test. The means of the latter two vignettes, seductive behavior and gender harassment, are not statistically significantly different ($p = .63$).

2 For ease of explanation, I present these data in reverse order from the actual survey, where they appeared as strongly agree to strongly disagree.

3 * = .05 and below
** = .01 and below
*** = .001 and below.

4 The fifth firm did not participate in the survey component of this study.

5 These are *perceptions* of organizational rules rather than an external legal analysis of whether the rules of the organization actually prohibit this behavior. However, as discussed in Chapter 5, employees at Gulf Stream, the onc firm without a sexual harassment policy, were the least likely to believe that conduct violated organizational rules, so I have some confidence that the respondents are thinking about the actual rules of the organization in answering the question.

6 While I only detail the cross-national results of the employee survey in this book, I also included two within-country vignettes on the surveys. Using the same model for these within-country vignettes (minus the nation variable), I found that employee perceptions of organizational rules was by far the most significant explanatory factor in individual understandings of illegality. In Austria, these vignettes included quid pro quo ($p = .009$) and sexual coercion ($p = 0.19$), and in the USA the far less severe examples of compliments (0.003) and a former relationship (.001). In each instance, the more an employee believed the conduct violated organizational rules, the more likely he or she was to also believe it was illegal.

7 Indeed, an attorney would be well advised to include this question in jury *voir dire*.

7 Conclusions

This study shows the fundamental importance of social context in leading to the understanding and implementation of law. Despite similar legal definitions, individuals and organizational decision makers interpreted law differently, through their own social context. The legal definition of sexual harassment is not a stable category; rather, it is interpreted and reinterpreted by individuals who exist in particular social contexts. This social context varies constitutively, orders and shapes the understanding of what law means and how it should be implemented. However, this study also shows that 'social context' is not a catch-all category. Studies attributing variation in law to 'social context' are overlooking at least three distinct conceptual categories within social context: the national context, the organizational context and the individual context. *Each* of these aspects of social context has the potential to influence the way law is understood and implemented.

This finding implies that variation in legal understandings and implementation may be misattributed to differences in legal systems. I found that factors from each element, the national context, the organizational context and individual differences, interact to generate variations in the perceptions of law. The contributions of *each* level have important public policy implications for both reformers and regulators.

The National Context

While similar legal words may dominate the global legal landscape, local cultural understandings provide meaning and largely determine the use of those words. Individuals within firms seek to make sense of the laws around them by understanding law through their national context. While the definition of Austrian and US sexual harassment was similar, for the most part, US managers placed sexual harassment within the context of risk, while Austrian managers tended to place sexual harassment within the context of US cultural dominance. In this detailed case study, we had very similar legal forms, but very different legal understandings.

This suggests that the success of current attempts to standardize new areas of commercial, criminal and human rights law will be intertwined with the national context. Parliamentary successes must be sustained by contextual interpretations long after the passing of the legal text. We should expect that the defining issues of old battles won in the passing of laws will again reappear when individuals give their own, contextual interpretations to the law.

The Organizational Context

It is not only the national context that leads to variation in the interpretation of similar law. Recent examinations of legal globalization tend to assume that the salient social context of law is the national or regional context. And rightly so: the national context is one way law is given meaning. However, law is also localized through the organizational, or corporate, context. National differences are important, but they are mediated by factors from the organizational context.

The organizational context provides a set of rules and norms from which organizational actors, such as employees and managers, interpret and enact law. This context shapes the ways that organizational decision makers implement law, the ways that employees understand the law and the strength of the influence of national context. Strikingly, I found that it was the perceptions of organizational rules, *rather than external law*, that were most important in explaining individual understandings of law. Further, it was found that, in at least one instance, organizational context was more important to the interpretation of sexual harassment law than was national context. Managers at the US multinational, Jet Stream, located in Austria with mostly Austrian employees, interpreted law in ways more similar than dissimilar to the US managers. I suggest that the three elements of social context have varying strength in influencing interpretations of law at various points in time, across various settings and among different individuals.

The Individual Context

Finally, often overlooked in legal studies, individual attitudes and socio-demographic characteristics profoundly influence the way that law is interpreted. Individuals vary in the degree to which they agree with regulation, and this influences whether or not they will see rule violations. While judges in the formal legal system have the task of interpreting the law, we know that most legal disputes never get before a judge. Instead, they are conceptualized and resolved in informal contexts, such as the corporation. Managers, employees, friends, neighbors, religious officials – *everyone* interacts with law and interprets it according to their own life's circumstances and beliefs.

While this study showed strong effects of ideological opposition to sex discrimination law in interpretations and support for the implementation of law, the empirical support for sociodemographic categories, such as sex, was far weaker. This is in contrast to the dominant focus of research into the definition of sexual harassment, as well as some court opinions utilizing the reasonable woman standard. This work asserts that women are more likely to define sexual harassment broadly than men. While this may very well be true, the present study shows that, like national context and organizational context, individual differences cannot be understood in isolation. *Individuals are part of complex and multi-layered social systems and where they live, where they work and who they are all interact to influence their interpretation of law.*

While our primary finding, described above, argues that each of the three levels of social context is fundamentally important to the interpretation and implementation of law, the more specific empirical findings from this study are summarized below, using examples from both the managerial level and the employee level.

There are National Differences in the Understandings of Similar Law

Managers and employees in the United States and Austria tended to express different understandings of sexual harassment law. As described in Chapter 4, managers in Austria were more likely to rely on the Legitimacy Challenge template in their understandings and implementation of law while, in the USA, managers were more likely to rely on a Risk Management template. Again, at the employee level, it was found that employees in Austria were less likely to identify conduct as illegal than were employees in the USA. However, these national differences did not carry through to employee support for punitive organizational action: US and Austrian employees were equally likely to support the dismissal of a 'harasser' in response to a particular vignette.

While clearly the nation, as a local site for the interpretation of law, is important to the cultural understanding of law, it is quite surprising that it is not *more* important. Given the tremendous differences in the legal systems and history of the USA and Austria, described in Chapters 2 and 3, we might have expected national site to far outweigh any other explanatory factor. This, of course, is the underlying assumption of much comparative law scholarship, but it was not found to be the case. As expressed in Chapter 6, there were strong, significant national differences in employee understandings of illegality, but they did not explain all of the variation in employee responses. Further, in considering managerial responses in Chapter 4, there were different tendencies of the US and Austrian managers, but national site did not explain all of the differences in managerial interpretations of sexual harassment law. Individuals determine illegality through their national context, but these interpretations are informed by other aspects of the social context.

The Organizational Context has a Role in Shifting Attention from one Set of National Laws to Another

Laws and organizations are not nationally bound, and this matters for understandings and interpretations of sexual harassment law. I found that, at the multinational Jet Stream, managers *chose* to focus on US law on the basis of factors from the organizational context. Because of this, their employees operate under a different set of policies, rhetoric and rules from those of the other Austrian employees in this study. Multinational firms are faced with conflicts of law issues every day, but, to the degree that the legal issue is constructed as an organizational problem, managers are particularly free to select their own set of regulatory rules. This finding is especially important in contexts of low state coercion, such as sexual harassment law.

There is a Cognitive Link between Informal Organizational Rule Structures and State Law

Employees look to the organization to determine what is illegal under national law. It was found that employees rely on their understandings of organizational prohibitions to understand state law. As regards employees, the more likely it is that an individual believes something is not allowed under the organization's rules, the more likely they also believe it is illegal under national law, and the more likely they will support punitive organizational action.

Considering the findings of organizational decision makers, in some instances managers relied on organizational standards of conduct, such as respect and courtesy to others, instead of the legal standards. Organizational norms were used by managers to regulate what might otherwise be regulated by sexual harassment law, although the regulation was enacted under the guise – and the legitimacy – of sexual harassment law. The more accessible concepts of respect and courtesy, readily available in the organizational context of the organizations, replaced the legal words found in sexual harassment policies or the law.

Individuals Sometimes Give Priority to the Normative Orderings of the Organization over State Law

It is striking that perceptions of organizational rules, *rather than perceptions of national law*, were most important in explaining individual support for punitive action. As recounted in Chapter 6, I found that individuals rely on their understandings of organizational rules in supporting or not supporting organizational action, while employee understandings of illegality under state law had no effect on support for punitive organizational action. Similarly, employees in firms that adopted a sexual harassment policy were less likely to invoke state law and to define conduct as illegal.

This link is also encouraged in the formal sexual harassment law of the USA. Recent Supreme Court decisions benefit organizations which develop their own rules and procedures regarding sexual harassment. Not only are courts encouraging organizations to develop their own rule systems regarding sexual harassment, they do so without serious ideological competition from the state. Where we might expect a court review and potential rejection of organizational ideology, federal sexual harassment law tends to defer to and incorporate organizational ideology into state law. Further, only very few of the sex discrimination cases are ever subject to legal review. While this is true in almost every type of legal dispute, it is exacerbated by a linked legal trend of requiring potential plaintiffs to exhaust the internal legal procedures of their employer before their case can proceed in court. I would expect this empirical finding to increase in importance over time in the USA.

Ideological Beliefs Influence the Understanding and Implementation of Law

As observed in Chapter 6, the ideological opposition to sex discrimination law in general fundamentally influenced whether employees recognized particular conduct as violating the law. Employees opposed to sex discrimination law were less likely to identify conduct as illegal under national law, and they were less likely to support punitive organizational action against the 'harasser'. While this finding appears to reflect common sense, the attitudes of individuals charged with interpreting law at the informal level are almost never considered in empirical studies of law, and rarely even conceptualized in legal theory. This finding suggests that, beyond sociodemographic characteristics such as sex, we should consider that individuals have different values and opinions and that this affects the ways that law is understood, implemented and disseminated.

Individual Actors are Selective (but Not Necessarily Purposive) in Utilizing Information from the Social Context in Understanding and Implementing Law

It was pointed out in Chapter 4 that the managerial templates used to interpret illegality reflect norms that are consistent with *organizational purposes*. Managerial understandings of law were intertwined with various assumptions of the national context in ways that either resisted and limited legal regulation or increased organizational control over employees. In the face of ambiguous law, organizational managers rely on those interpretations of illegality that are consistent with organizational purposes.

In sum, this study provides a detailed empirical study of how law is understood through three levels of the social context. However, rather than being a catch-all category, the social factors upon which individuals rely in their interpretations are associated with the individuals interpreting law, the organizational context of the interpretation and the national context – all aspects of the social context. Differences in understandings of similar law are explained by the various roles of these three distinct aspects of social context.

Appendix I Methods

In this appendix I further describe the methods used in selecting the organizational case studies, in gathering information within the firms and the implications of the methods I have used. The organizations are matched on the particular characteristics of size, industry and percentage of female workers, so the survey does not permit generalizations to pharmaceutical firms with large corporate sites, organizations in other industries or organizations with primarily male or primarily female employees. Larger corporate sites in the pharmaceutical industry tend to have well-established offices and employees dedicated to personnel issues, a well as in-house counsel, which is rarer in smaller firms. However, many of these US and Austrian managers worked at other (large) firms in the pharmaceutical industry, and drew on their earlier experiences during the interview.

Because the sample also controlled for industry, the results may not apply to firms outside the pharmaceutical industry. While sexual harassment law is not a legal issue particular to one industry, it is possible that there are norms within the organizational field of pharmaceuticals regarding the implementation of sexual harassment law.[1] This was not evident in the opinions expressed by the respondents, who never mentioned that the pharmaceutical industry was exceptional. There was nothing else in the data to suggest that the processes were industry-specific.

Organizations in this sample were also similar in gender composition. All of these organizations employed between 42 per cent and 60 per cent women. The findings from these organizations may not be generalizable to organizations that are predominantly male or predominantly female. Indeed, some researchers suggest that employees are less likely to perceive behavior as sexually harassing in male-dominated jobs (Konrad and Gutek, 1986; Gutek, 1985) and ethnographic research reflects the potential for male-dominated organizational cultures to be particularly discriminatory to women (Arriola, 1990). Although these researchers focus on the employee rather than manager perceptions of sexual harassment, it is at least theoretically plausible that these findings may not generalize to organizations strongly skewed on the gender composition of their employees.

Data Collection within the Organizations

Each interview lasted approximately one hour. In all but one instance, the interviews were taped and transcribed.[2] My goal as an interviewer was to elicit managerial understandings of sexual harassment within the context of the organization, which likely included aspects of the formal and informal constructions used by managers. The self-reported nature of the interviews raises questions of social desirability. It could be that the respondents wanted to place their firms in the most flattering light by exaggerating their commitment to sexual harassment law. To address this issue, participating organizations were specifically told that organizational compliance was not the goal of this study, in addition to being promised confidentiality. In encouraging the respondents to be honest, I reiterated that the goal of the interviews was to gain an understanding of how sexual harassment law is conceptualized, not whether it exists in the organizations. I read their responses carefully, looking not just for the overt text, but also for the subtext revealed in the way they related concepts and issues to one another. I found little evidence to suggest the respondents were consistently exaggerating their commitment to combating sexual harassment; in fact, many of the managers directly challenged sexual harassment law.

The second goal of data collection was to explore employee understandings of law. To meet this objective, I disseminated employee surveys. While employee interviews might reveal more detail in the ways employees understand sexual harassment law within the organization, I chose to rely on surveys because I had unfettered access to all employees, rather than a select group chosen by managers. Further, I increased the 'n' size by distributing surveys to all employees in each of the firms, increasing the potential for generalization.

Administration of the Survey

I distributed surveys to all employees through their mailboxes and these were returned by mail directly to me. The survey was either in English or German, depending on the site (Austrian sites received the German-version survey).[3] Each employee received two self-addressed, stamped envelopes and was instructed to use the small envelope to return the consent form (which was to be signed) and the large envelope to return the unsigned questionnaire. Approximately one week after initial distribution of the survey, I sent follow-up letters to all employees (in employee mailboxes), asking them to return their questionnaires if they had not already done so.

The overall response rate was 57 per cent, with a disproportionate number of women responding in every firm, but this was especially the case in Austria.

Recall that I report my findings net the effects of sex. The highest employee response rate came from Hudson, where 67.3 per cent returned the survey. The lowest response rate came from the other US domestic firm, Prairie, where 45 per cent of the respondents returned their survey. In my initial conversations with managers at Prairie, I was informed that the employees had recently been given several surveys concerning the organizational culture of the firm and that they might be tired of surveys, which might explain their comparatively low response rate.[4]

The Substance of the Questionnaire

I designed sexual harassment vignettes to assess employee understandings and applications of sexual harassment law. The vignettes compose the bulk of the questionnaire, which includes five vignettes of situations at work, followed by a series of questions relating to whether the vignette is an example of sexual harassment and what, if anything, the organization should do about it. Use of vignettes is common in sexual harassment research (for example, Cohen *et al.*, 1985; Fitzgerald and Hesson-McInnis, 1989; Baker *et al.*, 1990; Summers, 1991; Hunter and McClelland, 1991; Tata, 1993) and, although less common in cross-national research, there are examples of vignettes in this area as well (Sanders and Hamilton, 1992).

Since my research goal was to explore employee understandings of law and not what particulars of sexual harassment vignettes will increase the likelihood that employees will label conduct sexual harassment, I have held constant several aspects of interactions that other researchers have found important. First, the characters in the vignettes do not vary according to the gender of the actors (the male is the offender and the female is the recipient of the conduct) or the status of the actors (the male is of higher organizational status), both factors which would be likely to influence responses to the vignettes. In addition, all vignettes are set within the organization, on the premises. Respondents are asked to assume that all of the people in the situations are unmarried and that, unless specifically noted, none of the people have had prior romantic relationships with each other.

The vignettes do vary according to three types of harassment conceptualized by Gefland *et al.* (1995): gender harassment, unwanted sexual attention (including seductive behavior and sexual imposition) and sexual coercion (including sexual coercion and sexual bribery). There are five vignettes on each questionnaire.[5] Three are the same in the US and the Austrian surveys, and two are comparable within country.[6]

There are two primary dependent variables in the survey data analyis. The first is illegality, or whether employees believe the conduct described in the vignette is illegal. This is assessed, based on an ordinal rating of whether the vignette describes illegal behavior. The second is employee support for punitive organizational action (dismissal) against the protagonist described in the vignette.

The survey also contains questions designed to measure understandings of organizational rules and organizational context. After each vignette, employees rate the extent to which they believe conduct is prohibited by organizational rules. The survey also measures other aspects of organizational legal culture related to sex discrimination law, such as attentiveness to law and compliance.

Attitudes related to national context are measured specifically in questions regarding the rule of law, neutrality of law and valuation of liberty designed by Gibson and Calderia (1996). The English and translated German versions are adopted from the Euro-Barometer 38.0: European Court of Justice, Passive Smoking and Consumer Issues (1992) which was provided by the Inter-university Consortium for Political and Social Research (ICPSR). Attitudes toward anti-discrimination law are also measured on an ordinal scale. Finally, I measure national context itself through the proxy of nationality.

The survey also measured demographic characteristics of gender, age, race (USA only), nationality, employment status, length of time with the company, union membership, religion, education, political views, occupational function and gender composition of workgroup (USA only). I asked employees for their dispute history with the organization and the type of procedure used to resolve the dispute. Finally, I asked employees to identify sources of their knowledge about sexual harassment law (for example, managers, friends, media). Below, I describe the sociodemographic attributes in employees at the four firms participating in the survey.

Sociodemographic Attributes of Employees

While the sociodemographic attributes described below were tested for their effect on employee understandings and implementation of sexual harassment law, I further detail the employee differences in each of the firms below. The attributes of employees at Hudson, Prairie, Jet Stream and Gulf Stream are summarized in Table A.1. They only describe the employees who *actually responded* to the questionnaire, not all employees. This issue of selection bias is most noticeable in the percentage of female employees. In all but one firm, compared to men women responded disproportionately highly. While there was only a slight difference at Gulf Stream and Prairie, at Jet Stream this difference was substantial. Jet Stream employs 47 per cent females, but Jet Stream's respondents were 72 per cent female. I have reported my findings in earlier chapters taking into acount the effects of sex.

Table A.1 Demographic attributes within the firms (percentages)

	Hudson	Prairie	Jet Stream	Gulf Stream	Pr>Chi2
Gender (% female)	57	47	72	50	.04
Age[1]					
(18–30)	35	31	33	21	.26
(31–39)	23	40	43	29	
(40–68)	42	29	24	50	
Race or ethnicity[2]					
White, non-hispanic	88	80	n/a	n/a	.37
Political orientation[3]					
Left	4.35	18.18	12.96	8.33	.00
Moderate	34.78	45.45	70.37	70.83	
Right	60.87	36.36	16.67	20.83	
Religion					
Catholic	23	44	70	75	.00
other Christian	55	19	21	20	
Jewish	5	16	0	0	
Other	18	22	9	5	
Level of education					
Under high school/*matura*	0	0	7	8	.00
High school/*matura*	12	0	39	67	
University/trade	65	50	52	25	
Graduate	23	50	2	0	

Notes:

1 In other analyses, age is a continuous variable.

2 The category of race or ethnicity was not included on the Austrian survey.

3 Based on a scale ranging from 1 (left) to 10 (right). These data were recoded as 1–3 left, 4–6 moderate and 7–10 right. In other analyses, 'political orientation' remains a continuous variable.

There are some other differences among the firms. Most notable is nationality. This difference was part of the study design and, as expected, almost all of the respondents in the Austrian-based US multinationals are Austrian and almost all the respondents in the US domestic firms are US nationals. Reflecting national political differences, employees at the Austrian firms tended to fall into the 'moderate' category on a scale from 1 (left) to 10 (right) compared to employees at the US firms. This national difference was also reflected in the religion of respondents. Most respondents in Austria identify themselves as Catholic, while in the US-based firms there is more variation in self-identified religious affiliation. Finally, employees at the US firms tended to have higher levels of education than respondents at the firms in Austria.[7] This difference is likely due to the difference in primary functions at the firms. Hudson and Prairie had a larger focus on research and development, requiring employees with higher levels of education than the two US multinational firms, which focus on marketing and distribution.[8]

Organizational Climate

I now turn to employee impressions of the organizational climate of their firm, especially as it relates to sexual harassment and anti-discrimination law. I observed several nationality-based differences, but there are also some differences based on the particular organization (see Table A.2).

There were very few respondents in any of the firms identifying problems with sexual harassment. These problems did not necessarily occur while they were employed at the participating firms, but occurred within the last five years. The employees responding to the survey at Gulf Stream were the most likely to have experienced a sexual harassment problem, while respondents at Hudson were the most likely to have experienced a gender discrimination problem. When compared to employees at the other firms, employees tended to have disputes over issues other than discrimination most often at Hudson. These disputes centered primarily on salary, benefits and promotion. Like the sociodemographic characteristics, these variables were tested for their effects on the dependent variables and therefore were not included in the model explained in Chapter 6.

Variables not Included in the Quantitative Model

I also tested for the effect of other sociodemographic variables, including sex, age, political orientation, religion (Catholic/not Catholic), education and occupational function.[9] Considering the relationship between the demographic

Table A.2 Organizational disputes

	Prairie	Hudson	Jet Stream	Gulf Stream	Pr> Chi2
Had a problem with an employer regarding sexual harassment within the past 5 years (percentage of total respondents from that firm)	3	7	3	13	—
Had a problem with an employer regarding gender discrimination (not sexual harassment) within the past 5 years (percentage of total respondents from that firm)	3	11	5	4	—
Had a problem with an employer over non-discrimination issues including salary, promotion, working hours, work assignment, safety or health within the past 5 years (percentage of total respondents from that firm)	38	63	41	54	—

variables and employee understandings of illegality, I found that, in relation to the gender harassment vignette, only sex and age retained a statistical level of significance. Women were more likely to find the conduct illegal and, the older the employee, the more likely they were to find the conduct illegal. None of these variables obtain statistical significance on the seductive behavior vignette. I also tested for the role these sociodemographic variables play on employee support for punitive organizational action in the gender harassment, seductive behavior and sexual imposition vignettes. Only in the sexual imposition vignette did any variable reach statistical significance. In this model, men were slightly more likely to support punitive organizational action against a harasser.

I tested for an explanatory role for variables relating to the employee–employer relationship. First, I tested for a relationship between the dependent variables and whether an employee had a dispute with his or her employer over an issue of gender, sexual harassment or other type of discrimination. None of these variables was significant, with the exception of sex discrimination, regarding whether the employee supported discharge in the sexual imposition vignette. Individuals who had a dispute regarding sex discrimination were significantly less likely to support discharge in this vignette. I next tested for any relationships between employee disputes over non-discrimination issues including salary, promotion, hours, work assignments and health, and other issues. I also tested for a relationship between time with the company, worker attachment (whether the employee is likely to leave) and employment status (full-time or not). There were few significant relationships. I found that an 'other, non-discrimination' employment dispute was marginally related to defining illegality in the seductive behavior vignette. Employees with these disputes were slightly less likely to define the conduct as illegal. When considering employee support for dismissal, I found that, the more likely an employee was to leave their job, the less likely they were to support dismissal. Finally, I found that full-time employees were less likely to support dismissal than employees with other statuses in the gender harassment vignette.

Lastly, I tested for a relationship between whether the firm had a human resource office, understandings of illegality and support for dismissal. I did not find any significant relationships between having a human resource office and the dependent variables. Because of the weak relationship between these variables and the dependent variables, and no overriding theoretical concern in this exploration, these variables are not included in the model.

Notes

1 There was one widely reported instance of sexual harassment in the industry just before the interview process began, although it was not mentioned by any of the interviewees. The CEO of the Swedish pharmaceutical firm Astra was accused of sexual harassment, resulting in a damage payment by the company and the discharge of the CEO.

2 The CEO of the Austrian firm Alpen refused to be tape-recorded. I took detailed notes during the interview, and the manager's responses were recreated as accurately and completely as possible. Quotations used from this interview are based on my notes.

3 In Austria, the survey was given in German, and in the United States, it was given in English. The survey was written in English and pretested. On the basis of feedback, it was revised and then translated into German. Using a separate translator, it was translated back into English. Differences between the English and German versions were then refined to ensure the same meaning in both surveys. Finally, two bilingual individuals completed the questionnaire in both English and German, noting any differences, which were again refined.

4 The surveys at Jet Stream and Gulf Stream were conducted in two waves. At Jet Stream, a random sample of one-third of the employees were given questionnaires and, a few months later, questionnaires were distributed to the remaining two-thirds. At Gulf Stream, two waves were conducted, one year apart. In the first wave, a 38 per cent response rate was obtained. This may be due to the fact that they were distributed in August, when many of

the employees were on vacation. Because of the comparatively low response rate, when I next returned to Austria a second wave of surveys was distributed to employees that had not previously responded. Males were more likely to respond in the second wave than in the first. This increased the total response rate to 53.3 per cent. In testing for differences between wave 1 and wave 2 on the dependent variables, no significant differences were found in the likelihood that employees would invoke a legal frame in their support of internal punishment of rule-breakers or in support of the mobilization of law.

5 I randomly varied the order of the sexual harassment vignettes in three versions of the survey (in both English and German) which were given to employees. This was done to measure any bias caused by the order of the vignettes in employee responses. In testing for a significant relationship between the survey version and the dependent variables, no significant relationships were found.

6 The German version includes two vignettes on sexual coercion (including an example of quid pro quo harassment and sexual bribery) which are replaced in the English version by an example of unwanted sexual attention and gender harassment.

7 The US and Austrian education systems are *not* comparable, and these data are more useful cross-nationally in an ordinal context. Among other differences, a 'matura' degree represents the completion of comprehensive qualifying exams at the end of high school in Austria, which reflects a higher status than a high school degree in the USA.

8 I also observed differences in the occupational function of the employees at each firm. Employees in the US firms are more likely than Austrian-based employees to be involved in research and development as their primary occupational function. Employees in Austria are slightly more likely to have a managerial function or to be involved in marketing.

9 I used dummy variables for the categories of manager, research and development, manufacturing and production, clerical and marketing.

Appendix II Employee Opinions about Law Survey

Part I: General Attitudes

Individuals can have very different views of the importance of law in general and anti-discrimination law in particular. I would like to get your opinion. Please indicate the degree to which you agree or disagree with the following statements by circling the number according to whether you:

1 Strongly Agree, 2 Agree Somewhat, 3 Are Undecided, 4 Disagree Somewhat, or 5 Strongly Disagree.

A. General Attitudes About Law (circle the number that best reflects your answer)

1. It is better to live in an orderly society than to allow people so much freedom that they can become disruptive.
Strongly Agree 1 2 3 4 5 Strongly Disagree

2. If a person doesn't particularly agree with a law, it is all right for them to break it if they are careful not to get caught.
Strongly Agree 1 2 3 4 5 Strongly Disagree

3. My interests are rarely represented in the law.
Strongly Agree 1 2 3 4 5 Strongly Disagree

4. Usually law reflects the views of those who want to control me.
Strongly Agree 1 2 3 4 5 Strongly Disagree

5. Companies that have rules for promotion based on seniority are more fair than companies that promote based on performance.
Strongly Agree 1 2 3 4 5 Strongly Disagree

6. I agree with the laws to protect women against discrimination.
Strongly Agree 1 2 3 4 5 Strongly Disagree

7. It is much better for every one involved if the man earns the money and the woman takes care of the home and children.

Strongly Agree 1 2 3 4 5 Strongly Disagree

8. Laws against discrimination seem silly to me.

Strongly Agree 1 2 3 4 5 Strongly Disagree

9. Sexual harassment laws do more harm than good.

Strongly Agree 1 2 3 4 5 Strongly Disagree

10. Laws against sex discrimination are necessary in today's society.

Strongly Agree 1 2 3 4 5 Strongly Disagree

11. Laws against sex discrimination serve a useful purpose in organizations.

Strongly Agree 1 2 3 4 5 Strongly Disagree

B. Company Focus on Law

Companies vary in the degree to which they treat employees fairly and the degree to which they discriminate or do not discriminate against women. In this section, I have listed a series of statements related to these topics. Considering your company, please indicate the degree to which you agree or disagree with the following statements.

12. Managers strictly follow legal standards.

Strongly Agree 1 2 3 4 5 Strongly Disagree

13. Managers are not concerned with complying with anti-discrimination law for women.

Strongly Agree 1 2 3 4 5 Strongly Disagree

14. Managers are very concerned with complying with sexual harassment laws.

Strongly Agree 1 2 3 4 5 Strongly Disagree

15. It is obvious by managers' actions that they try to comply with equal employment laws.

Strongly Agree 1 2 3 4 5 Strongly Disagree

16. Managers are biased against female employees.

Strongly Agree 1 2 3 4 5 Strongly Disagree

17. A major concern for managers is complying with anti-discrimination law for women.

Strongly Agree 1 2 3 4 5 Strongly Disagree

18. Managers promote males much more readily than females.

Strongly Agree 1 2 3 4 5 Strongly Disagree

19. My company gives out rewards to those who deserve them, regardless of their gender.

Strongly Agree 1 2 3 4 5 Strongly Disagree

20. In my company, everybody applies anti-discrimination policies for women in the same way.

Strongly Agree 1 2 3 4 5 Strongly Disagree

Part II: Hypothetical Situations at Work

Next, I would like your reaction to specific situations that sometimes occur at work. Each situation should be considered separately. Assume that all of the people in the situations are unmarried and that none of the people have had prior sexual relationships with each other. According to your opinion, please answer the questions following the situations:

Situation 1

Ms. Abel is the only female manager in her department at Firm X. Mr. Bauer, her supervisor, often tells Ms. Abel that she has no business being in thc management department and that she belongs home in the kitchen. When Ms. Abel arrives at the office, her supervisor says, "Why do you bother to come to work? Only men belong here." Ms. Abel asked Mr. Bauer to stop making these statements.

1. Under United States law, I think Mr. Bauer's behavior would be considered:

1	2	3	4	5
Absolutely Legal	Probably Legal	Probably Illegal	Absolutely Illegal	Don't Know

2. Under the official rules governing my workplace, I think Mr. Bauer's behavior would be:

1	2	3	4	5
Absolutely Allowed	Probably Allowed	Probably Forbidden	Absolutely Forbidden	Don't Know

3. How socially appropriate is Mr. Bauer's behavior?

1	2	3	4	5
Absolutely Appropriate	Probably Appropriate	Probably Inappropriate	Absolutely Inappropriate	Don't Know

4. Ms. Abel is considering many reactions to Mr. Bauer's behavior. Please rate each potential response by Ms. Abel based on how strongly you agree she should make it.

strongly agree			strongly disagree	
__1	__2	__3	__4	Ignore Mr. Bauer's behavior.
__1	__2	__3	__4	Make of joke of Mr. Bauer's behavior in public.
__1	__2	__3	__4	Have another manager tell Mr. Bauer to stop his behavior.
__1	__2	__3	__4	Make a complaint to a union representative.
__1	__2	__3	__4	Make a complaint to the EEOC.
__1	__2	__3	__4	Hire a lawyer to sue Mr. Bauer.

5. Ms. Abel complains to her company about the conduct of Mr. Bauer. Please rate each potential response by the company towards Mr. Bauer based on how strongly you agree with it.

strongly agree			strongly disagree	
__1	__2	__3	__4	Do nothing against Mr. Bauer.
__1	__2	__3	__4	Do nothing against Mr. Bauer, but ask him to seek psychological counseling.
__1	__2	__3	__4	Tell Mr. Bauer to change his behavior toward Ms. Abel.
__1	__2	__3	__4	Record Mr. Bauer's actions as negative in his personnel file.
__1	__2	__3	__4	Transfer Mr. Bauer to another department in the company.
__1	__2	__3	__4	Fire Mr. Bauer.

6. Ms. Abel complains to her company about the conduct of Mr. Bauer. Please rate each potential response by the company towards Ms. Abel based on how strongly you agree with it.

strongly agree			strongly disagree	
__1	__2	__3	__4	Do nothing against Ms. Abel.
__1	__2	__3	__4	Do nothing against Ms. Abel, but ask her to seek psychological counselling.
__1	__2	__3	__4	Tell Ms. Abel to change her behavior toward Mr. Bauer.
__1	__2	__3	__4	Record Ms. Abel's actions as negative in her personnel file.

__1 __2 __3 __4 Transfer Ms. Abel to another department in the company.
__1 __2 __3 __4 Fire Ms. Abel.

7. Do you consider this situation to be an example of sexual harassment?

___Yes. ___No.

Comments: ____
____
____
__________.

Situation 2

Ms. Ebner is the only female manager in her department at Firm X. Her supervisor Mr. Frank, often talks about every detail of Ms. Ebner's physical appearance. For example, Mr. Frank has asked Ms. Ebner what bra size she wears, and whether she wears underwear. Ms. Ebncr has asked Mr. Frank to stop this behavior.

1. Under United States law, I think Mr. Frank's behavior would be considered:

1	2	3	4	5
Absolutely Legal	Probably Legal	Probably Illegal	Absolutely Illegal	Don't Know

2. Under the official rules governing my workplace, I think Mr. Frank's behavior would be:

1	2	3	4	5
Absolutely Allowed	Probably Allowed	Probably Forbidden	Absolutely Forbidden	Don't Know

3. How socially appropriate is Mr. Frank's behavior?

1	2	3	4	5
Absolutely Appropriate	Probably Appropriate	Probably Inappropriate	Absolutely Inappropriate	Don't Know

4. Ms. Ebner is considering many reactions to Mr. Frank's behavior. Please rate each potential response by Ms. Ebner based on how strongly you agree she should make it.

strongly agree ... strongly disagree

__1 __2 __3 __4 Ignore Mr. Frank's behavior.
__1 __2 __3 __4 Make of joke of Mr. Frank's behavior in public.
__1 __2 __3 __4 Have another manager tell Mr. Frank to stop his behavior.

__1 __2 __3 __4 Make a complaint to a union representative.
__1 __2 __3 __4 Make a complaint to the Equal Employment Opportunity Commission.
__1 __2 __3 __4 Hire a lawyer to sue Mr. Frank.

5. Ms. Ebner complains to her company about the conduct of Mr. Frank. Please rate each potential response by the company towards Mr. Frank based on how strongly you agree with it.

strongly agree — strongly disagree

__1 __2 __3 __4 Do nothing against Mr. Frank.
__1 __2 __3 __4 Do nothing against Mr. Frank, but ask him to seek psychological counseling.
__1 __2 __3 __4 Tell Mr. Frank to change his behavior toward Ms. Ebner.
__1 __2 __3 __4 Record Mr. Frank's actions as negative in his personnel file.
__1 __2 __3 __4 Transfer Mr. Frank to another department in the company.
__1 __2 __3 __4 Fire Mr. Frank.

6. Ms. Ebner complains to her company about the conduct of Mr. Frank. Please rate each potential response by the company towards Ms. Ebner based on how strongly you agree with it.

strongly agree — strongly disagree

__1 __2 __3 __4 Do nothing against Ms. Ebner.
__1 __2 __3 __4 Do nothing against Ms. Ebner, but ask her to seek psychological counseling.
__1 __2 __3 __4 Tell Ms. Ebner to change her behavior toward Mr. Frank.
__1 __2 __3 __4 Record Ms. Ebner's actions as negative in her personnel file.
__1 __2 __3 __4 Transfer Ms. Ebner to another department in the company.
__1 __2 __3 __4 Fire Ms. Ebner.

7. Do you consider this situation to be an example of sexual harassment?

___ Yes. ___ No.

Comments: ____
____.

Situation 3

Mr. Gruber told his secretary, Ms. Hoffman, that the dress she was wearing looked particularly nice on her to which she replied, "Thank you" but acted embarrassed. Mr. Gruber often compliments Ms. Hoffman on her clothing or a new haircut and she always has the same response.

1. Under United States law, I think Mr. Gruber's behavior would be considered:

1	2	3	4	5
Absolutely Legal	Probably Legal	Probably Illegal	Absolutely Illegal	Don't Know

2. Under the official rules governing my workplace, I think Mr. Gruber's behavior would be:

1	2	3	4	5
Absolutely Allowed	Probably Allowed	Probably Forbidden	Absolutely Forbidden	Don't Know

3. How socially appropriate is Mr. Gruber's behavior?

1	2	3	4	5
Absolutely Appropriate	Probably Appropriate	Probably Inappropriate	Absolutely Inappropriate	Don't Know

4. Ms. Hoffman is considering many reactions to Mr. Gruber's behavior. Please rate each potential response by Ms. Hoffman based on how strongly you agree she should make it.

strongly agree			strongly disagree	
__1	__2	__3	__4	Ignore Mr. Gruber's behavior.
__1	__2	__3	__4	Make of joke of Mr. Gruber's behavior in public.
__1	__2	__3	__4	Have another manager tell Mr. Gruber to stop his behavior.
__1	__2	__3	__4	Make a complaint to a union representative.
__1	__2	__3	__4	Make a complaint to the Equal Employment Opportunity Commission.
__1	__2	__3	__4	Hire a lawyer to sue Mr. Gruber.

5. Ms. Hoffman complains to her company about the conduct of Mr. Gruber. Please rate each potential response by the company towards Mr. Gruber based on how strongly you agree with it.

strongly agree			strongly disagree	
__1	__2	__3	__4	Do nothing against Mr. Gruber.

__ 1 __2 __3 __4 Do nothing against Mr. Gruber, but ask him to seek psychological counseling.
__ 1 __2 __3 __4 Tell Mr. Gruber to change his behavior toward Ms. Hoffman.
__ 1 __2 __3 __4 Record Mr. Gruber's actions as negative in his personnel file.
__ 1 __2 __3 __4 Transfer Mr. Gruber to another department in the company.
__ 1 __2 __3 __4 Fire Mr. Gruber.

6. Ms. Hoffman complains to her company about the conduct of Mr. Gruber. Please rate each potential response by the company towards Ms. Hoffman based on how strongly you agree with it.

strongly agree — strongly disagree

__ 1 __2 __3 __4 Do nothing against Ms. Hoffman.
__ 1 __2 __3 __4 Do nothing against Ms. Hoffman, but ask her to seek psychological counselling.
__ 1 __2 __3 __4 Tell Ms. Hoffman to change her behavior toward Mr. Gruber.
__ 1 __2 __3 __4 Record Ms. Hoffman's actions as negative in her personnel file.
__ 1 __2 __3 __4 Transfer Ms. Hoffman to another department in the company.
__ 1 __2 __3 __4 Fire Ms. Hoffman.

7. Do you consider this situation to be an example of sexual harassment?

___ Yes. ___ No.

Comments: ____

____.

Situation 4

Mr. Jung and Ms. Kaufman dated outside of the workplace for six months. Mr. Jung is Ms. Kaufman's supervisor. While they were both satisfied with their relationship while dating, they recently ended their relationship. Mr. Jung still includes Ms. Kaufman in department meetings and her performance reviews have remained the same, but Ms. Kaufman feels Mr. Jung is cold to her, and is less likely to invite her socially to lunch or to socialize with her at company functions. Ms. Kaufman complains to her employer about this.

1. Under United States law, I think Mr. Jung's behavior would be considered:

1	2	3	4	5
Absolutely Legal	Probably Legal	Probably Illegal	Absolutely Illegal	Don't Know

2. Under the official rules governing my workplace, I think Mr. Jung's behavior would be:

1	2	3	4	5
Absolutely Allowed	Probably Allowed	Probably Forbidden	Absolutely Forbidden	Don't Know

3. How socially appropriate is Mr. Jung's behavior?

1	2	3	4	5
Absolutely Appropriate	Probably Appropriate	Probably Inappropriate	Absolutely Inappropriate	Don't Know

4. Ms. Kaufman is considering many reactions to Mr. Jung's behavior. Please rate each potential response by Ms. Kaufman based on how strongly you agree she should make it.

strongly agree			strongly disagree	
__1	__2	__3	__4	Ignore Mr. Jung's behavior.
__1	__2	__3	__4	Make of joke of Mr. Jung's behavior in public.
__1	__2	__3	__4	Have another manager tell Mr. Jung to stop his behavior.
__1	__2	__3	__4	Make a complaint to a union representative.
__1	__2	__3	__4	Make a complaint to the Equal Employment Opportunity Commission.
__1	__2	__3	__4	Hire a lawyer to sue Mr. Jung.

5. Ms. Kaufman complains to her company about the conduct of Mr. Jung. Please rate each potential response by the company towards Mr. Jung based on how strongly you agree with it.

strongly agree			strongly disagree	
__1	__2	__3	__4	Do nothing against Mr. Jung.
__1	__2	__3	__4	Do nothing against Mr. Jung, but ask him to seek psychological counseling.
__1	__2	__3	__4	Tell Mr. Jung to change his behavior toward Ms. Kaufman.
__1	__2	__3	__4	Record Mr. Jung's actions as negative in his personnel file.
__1	__2	__3	__4	Transfer Mr. Jung to another department in the company.
__1	__2	__3	__4	Fire Mr. Jung.

6. Ms. Kaufman complains to her company about the conduct of Mr. Jung. Please rate each potential response by the company towards Ms. Kaufman based on how strongly you agree with it.

strongly agree			strongly disagree	
__1	__2	__3	__4	Do nothing against Ms. Kaufman.
__1	__2	__3	__4	Do nothing against Ms. Kaufman, but ask her to seek psychological counselling.
__1	__2	__3	__4	Tell Ms. Kaufman to change her behavior toward Mr. Jung.
__1	__2	__3	__4	Record Ms. Kaufman's actions as negative in her personnel file.
__1	__2	__3	__4	Transfer Ms. Kaufman to another department in the company.
__1	__2	__3	__4	Fire Ms. Kaufman.

7. Do you consider this situation to be an example of sexual harassment?

___Yes. ___No.

Comments: ____

____.

Situation 5

Mr. Lang found his secretary, Ms. Meyer alone in the office. Although they did not have a sexual relationship with each other, he grabbed her breasts against her will.

1. Under United States law, I think Mr. Lang's behavior would be considered:

1	2	3	4	5
Absolutely Legal	Probably Legal	Probably Illegal	Absolutely Illegal	Don't Know

2. Under the official rules governing my workplace, I think Mr. Lang's behavior would be:

1	2	3	4	5
Absolutely Allowed	Probably Allowed	Probably Forbidden	Absolutely Forbidden	Don't Know

3. How socially appropriate is Mr. Lang's behavior?

1	2	3	4	5
Absolutely Appropriate	Probably Appropriate	Probably Inappropriate	Absolutely Inappropriate	Don't Know

4. Ms. Meyer is considering many reactions to Mr. Lang's behavior. Please rate each potential response by Ms. Meyer based on how strongly you agree she should make it.

strongly agree			strongly disagree	
__1	__2	__3	__4	Ignore Mr. Lang's behavior.
__1	__2	__3	__4	Make of joke of Mr. Lang's behavior in public.
__1	__2	__3	__4	Have another manager tell Mr. Lang to stop his behavior.
__1	__2	__3	__4	Make a complaint to a union representative.
__1	__2	__3	__4	Make a complaint to the Equal Employment Opportunity Commission.
__1	__2	__3	__4	Hire a lawyer to sue Mr. Lang.

5. Ms. Meyer complains to her company about the conduct of Mr. Lang. Please rate each potential response by the company towards Mr. Lang based on how strongly you agree with it.

strongly agree			strongly disagree	
__1	__2	__3	__4	Do nothing against Mr. Lang.
__1	__2	__3	__4	Do nothing against Mr. Lang, but ask him to seek psychological counseling.
__1	__2	__3	__4	Tell Mr. Lang to change his behavior toward Ms. Meyer.
__1	__2	__3	__4	Record Mr. Lang's actions as negative in his personnel file.
__1	__2	__3	__4	Transfer Mr. Lang to another department in the company.
__1	__2	__3	__4	Fire Mr. Lang.

6. Ms. Meyer complains to her company about the conduct of Mr. Lang. Please rate each potential response by the company towards Ms. Meyer based on how strongly you agree with it.

strongly agree			strongly disagree	
__1	__2	__3	__4	Do nothing against Ms. Meyer.
__1	__2	__3	__4	Do nothing against Ms. Meyer, but ask her to seek psychological counselling.
__1	__2	__3	__4	Tell Ms. Meyer to change her behavior toward Mr. Lang.
__1	__2	__3	__4	Record Ms. Meyer's actions as negative in her personnel file.

__1 __2 __3 __4 Transfer Ms. Meyer to another department in the company.
__1 __2 __3 __4 Fire Ms. Meyer.

7. Do you consider this situation to be an example of sexual harassment?
___ Yes. ___ No.
Comments: ____
____.

Part III: Sources of Information

1. Please check all of the following sources from which you have learned something about *United States'* sexual harassment law.

___ From a special anti-discrimination program in my company.
___ From a special diversity program in my company.
___ From the personnel department or employee in my company.
___ From a written policy or rule in my company.
___ From my union.
___ From a manager.
___ From the news media.
___ From my own or a friend's experience with sexual harassment.
___ Other: ______________________________________.
___ I have never heard of the *US's* sexual harassment law.

Part IV: Problems at Work

1. Please think back to problems you personally have had with your employer(s) over things like salary, promotion, discrimination, etc. From the list below, please check each type of problem you have had at work during the past five years. Check each problem you have had in column A and each problem you have had in column B.

Column A

___ salary and/or benefits
___ promotion
___ working hours
___ work assignment
___ safety or health
___ something else, please specify: ____________.

Column B

___ Discrimination (please check type):
___ age ___ disability ___ race or ethnicity
___ gender (anti-discrimination)
___ religion
___ sexual harassment
___ something else, please specify: ____________.

IF YOU DID *NOT* TICK ANY ITEMS IN COLUMN B, PLEASE SKIP TO THE END OF THE SURVEY AND COMPLETE PART V, 'DEMOGRAPHIC INFORMATION'.
IF YOU *DID* TICK ONE OR MORE ITEMS IN COLUMN B, PLEASE CONTINUE WITH QUESTION 2.

2. Of those problems listed in column B, which did you most recently experience?

___ discrimination (please tick type):
 ___ age ___ disability ___ race or ethnicity ___ gender (anti-discrimination)
 ___ religion
 ___ sexual harassment
 ___ something else, please specify: ____________________.

3. Did you have any sort of meeting or hearing about this problem with your company?

___ Yes. With whom (e.g. supervisor, human resources officer) ____________.
___ No.

4. What procedures were used to finally reach a resolution to this problem (hearing, formal complaint, informal discussions with manager, etc.)?

____

____

___ No resolution reached.

5. How satisfied were you with the resolution of your problem?

1	2	3	4	5
Very Satisfied	Somewhat Satisfied	Somewhat Dissatisfied	Very Dissatisfied	Problem Unresolved

6. Compared to what you expected to receive from your experience, please rate your outcome:

1	2	3	4
Better than Expected	As Expected	Worse than Expected	Problem Unresolved

7. How fair were the procedures used to handle your problem?

1	2	3	4
Very Fair	Somewhat Fair	Somewhat Unfair	Very Unfair

PLEASE TURN TO THE LAST PAGE TO COMPLETE THE SURVEY

Part V: Demographic Information

1. Sex: ___ Male ___ Female
2. Age: ________.
3. Race: ___ White ___ African-American
 ___ Hispanic, white ___ Hispanic, non-white
 ___ Asian-American ___Other: ____________.
4. Employment status: ___ Full-time ___ Part-time ___ Consultant ___ Other: _________.
5. Length of time with this company ______ years.
6. How likely are you to make a genuine effort to find a new job with another employer within the next year? (Tick one):
___ Very Likely ___ Somewhat Likely ___ Not at all Likely.
7. Are you a member of a trade union?: ___ Yes ___ No.
8. Nationality: ___ United States ___Austrian ___ Other EU (please specify) ______________ Other: ______________.
9. Religion: ________________.
10. Education: Highest grade/level of school completed: ________________.
11. In political matters people talk of 'the left' and 'the right'. How would you place your views on this scale?

LEFT 1 2 3 4 5 6 7 8 9 10 RIGHT

12. Occupational function (please tick the *one* function that best describes what you do at work):

___ Research and Development
___ Human Resources/Personnel
___ Production/Manufacturing
___ Regulatory Affairs
___ Product Management
___ Sales/Marketing
___ Housekeeping/Maintenance
___ Quality Control/Assurance
___ Accounting/Purchasing
___ Engineering
___ Corporate Management
___ Manufacturing Management
___ Administrative support (Secretary, Clerical)
___ Legal

13. My workgroup (the individuals with whom I work the closest, such as a long-term project group, section or division) is (choose one):

1	2	3
Mostly Male	About Equally Male and Female	Mostly Female

THANK YOU FOR YOUR TIME AND EFFORT IN COMPLETING THIS SURVEY.

Bibliography

Abzug, Rikki and Stephen Mezias (1993), 'The Fragmented State and Due Process Protections in Organizations: the Case of Comparable Worth', *Organization Science*, 4(3), 433–53.

Aeberhard-Hodges, Jane (1996), 'Sexual Harassment in Employment: Recent Judicial and Arbitral Trends', *International Labour Review*, 135(5), 499–533.

Appelt, Erna M. (1998), 'Women in the Austrian Economy', in Anton Pelinka, Guenter Bischof and Erika Thurner (eds), *Contemporary Austrian Studies*, New Brunswick: Transaction Publishers.

Arriola, Elvia (1990), ' "What's the Big Deal?" Women in the New York City Construction Industry and Sexual Harassment Law, 1970–1985', *Columbia Human Rights Law Review*, 22, 21–71.

Baker, Douglas, David E. Terpstra and B. Culter (1990), 'Perceptions of Sexual Harassment: A Re-examination of Gender Differences', *The Journal of Psychology*, 124(4), 409–16.

Barker, Sally E. and Loretta K. Haggard (1992), 'A Labor Union's Duties and Potential Liabilities Arising Out of Coworker Complaints of Sexual Harassment', *Saint Louis University Public Law Review*, 11, 135–56.

Bei, Neda and Renate Novak (1997), 'Frauen und Recht-Rechtswissenschaft', in *Handbuch der Frauenrechte*, Vienna: Ulrike Aichorn, and New York: Springer Verlag.

Bernstein, Anita (1994), 'Law, Culture and Harassment', *University of Pennsylvania Law Review*, 142, 1227–311.

—— (1997), 'Treating Sexual Harassment With Respect', *Harvard Law Review*, 111, 446–527.

Bird, Robert C. (1997), 'More Than a Congressional Joke: A Fresh Look at the Legislative History of the Sex Discrimination of the 1964 Civil Rights Act', *William and Mary Journal of Women and the Law*, 3, 137–61.

Blumberg, Abraham S. (1967), 'The Practice of Law as a Confidence Game: Organizational Cooptation of a Profession', *Law & Society Review*, 1(2), 15.

Boiarsky, Carolyn, Laurel Grove, Barbara Northrop, Marianne Phillips, Felicity Myers and Patricia Earnest (1995), 'Women in Technical/Scientific

Professions: Results of Two National Surveys', *IEEE Transactions on Professional Communication*, 38(2), 68–76.

Bumiller, Kristin (1987), 'Victims in the Shadow of the Law: A Critique of the Model of Legal Protection', *Signs: Journal of Women in Culture and Society*, 12(3), 421–39.

Cahill, Mia (1996a), 'Sexual Harassment in the International Context', Seminar Series presented to the Vienna Women's Initiative Conferences, United States Embassy, Vienna, Austria, Spring/Summer.

—— (1996b), 'The Illusion of Precedent: The Construction of Sexual Harassment Law in Austria', paper presented to the 1996 Law & Society Association Annual Meeting and RCSL Joint Meetings on Globalization and the Quest for Justice, Glasgow, Scotland, 10–13 July.

—— (1999), 'Enacting the Law: The Role of Cultural Norms in the Legal Understandings of Organizational Actors', paper presented to the 1999 Law & Society Annual Meeting, Chicago, May.

Carter, Victoria A. (1992), 'Working on Dignity: EC Initiatives on Sexual Harassment in the Workplace', *Northwestern Journal of International Law & Business*, 12 (Winter), 431–53.

Cohen, Aaron Groff and Barbara A. Gutek (1985), 'Dimensions of Perceptions of Social-Sexual Behavior in a Work Setting', *Sex Roles*, 13(5/6), 317–27.

Collins, Eliza G.C. and Timothy B. Blodgett (1981), 'Some See It... Some Won't', *Harvard Business Review* (March–April), 76–96.

Collins, Evelyn (1996), 'European Union Sexual Harassment Policy', in Amy Elman (ed.), *Sexual Politics and the European Union: The New Feminist Challenge*, Oxford: Berghahn Books.

Crenshaw, Kimberle (1992), 'Race, Gender and Sexual Harassment', *Southern California Law Review*, 65, 1467–76.

Deitz-Uhler, B. and A. Murrell (1992), 'College Students' Perceptions of Sexual Harassment: Are Gender Differences Decreasing?', *Journal of College Student Development*, 33, 540–46.

DeJean, Joan (1993), 'Exporting America: Can "Sexual Harassment" Exist in France?', *French Politics and Society*, 11(3), 47–57.

Dolkart, Jane L. (1994), 'Hostile Environment Harassment: Equality, Objectivity, and the Shaping of Legal Standards', *Emory Law Journal*, 43 (Winter), 151–244.

Earle, Beverley H. and Gerald A. Madek (1993), 'An International Perspective on Sexual Harassment Law', *Law and Inequality*, 12(1), 43–91.

Edelman, Lauren (1990), 'Legal Environments and Organizational Governance: The Expansion of Due Process in the American Workplace', *American Journal of Sociology*, 95(6), 1401–40.

—— (1992), 'Legal Ambiguity and Symbolic Structures: Organizational

Mediation of Civil Rights Law', *American Journal of Sociology*, 97(6), 1531–76.

—— (1999), 'Constructed Legalities: Socio-Legal Fields and the Endogeneity of Law', in Walter W. Powell and Daniel Jones (eds), *Bending the Bars of the Iron Cage: Institutional Dynamics and Processes*, Chicago: University of Chicago Press.

Edelman, Lauren and Mark Suchman (1997), 'The Legal Environments of Organizations', *Annual Review of Sociology*, 23, 479–515.

Ehrenreich, Nancy S. (1990), 'Pluralist Myths and Powerless Men: The Ideology of Reasonableness in Sexual Harassment Law', *Yale Law Journal*, 99(6), 1117–234.

Elman, R. Amy (1996a), 'Feminism and Legislative Redress: Sexual Harassment in Sweden and the United States', *Women and Politics*, 16(3), 1–26.

—— (1996b), *Sexual Subordination and State Intervention: Comparing Sweden and the United States*, Providence and Oxford: Berghahn.

—— (2000), 'Sexual Harassment Policy: Sweden in European Context', Paper presented at the Twelfth International Conference of Europeanists, Chicago, 30 March–1 April.

Engel, David (1984), 'The Oven Bird's Song: Insiders, Outsiders and Personal Injuries in an American Community', *Law & Society Review*, 18, 551–82.

Engel, David and Frank Munger (1996), 'Rights, Remembrance and the Reconciliation of Difference', *Law & Society Review*, 30(1), 7–53.

Epp, Charles, R. (1998a), 'The Rights Revolution', Chicago: University of Chicago Press.

—— (1998b), 'Litigation Stories: Official Perceptions of Lawsuits Against Local Governments', paper presented at the 1998 Annual Meeting of the Law and Society Association, Aspen, Colorado.

Erlanger, Howard S., Elizabeth Chambliss and Marygold S. Melli (1987), 'Participation and Flexibility in Informal Processes: Cautions from the Divorce Context', *Law & Society Review*, 21, 585.

Ewick, Patricia and Susan Silbey (1992), 'Conformity, Contestation and Resistance: An Account of Legal Consciousness', *New England Law Review*, 26, 731–49.

—— (1998), *The Common Place of Law: Stories from Everyday Life*, Chicago: University of Chicago Press.

Farley, Lin (1978), *Sexual Shakedown*, New York: McGraw-Hill.

Feary, Vaughana Macy (1994), 'Sexual Harassment: Why the Corporate World Still Doesn't "Get It"', *Journal of Business Ethics*, 13, 649–62.

Felstiner, William L.F., Richard L. Abel and Austin Sarat (1980), 'The Emergence and Transformation of Disputes: Naming, Blaming, Claiming . . .', *Law & Society Review*, 15, 631–54.

Fitzgerald, Louise F. and Matthew Hesson-McInnis (1989), 'The Dimensions of Sexual Harassment: A Structural Analysis', *Journal of Vocational Behavior*, 35, 309–26.

Fitzgerald, Louise and Sandra L. Shullman (1993), 'Sexual Harassment: A Research Analysis and Agenda for the 1990s', *Journal of Vocational Behavior*, 42, 5–27.

Fligstein, Neil (1990), *The Transformation of Corporate Control*, Cambridge, MA: Harvard University Press.

—— (1985), 'The Spread of the Multidivisional Form among Large Firms, 1919–1979', *American Sociological Review*, 50 (June), 377–91.

Frazier, Patricia A., Caroline C. Cochran and Andrea M. Olson (1995), 'Social Science Research on Lay Definitions of Sexual Harassment', *Journal of Social Issues*, 51(1), 21–37.

Frederickson, Caroline (1995), 'Freedom of Contract and the Remedy of Forced Hiring: A Comparative Assessment of German and American Anti-Discrimination Law', *Journal of Law and Policy*, 4(1), 1–28.

Galanter, Marc (1999), 'An Oil Strike in Hell: Contemporary Legends About the Civil Justice System', *Arizona Law Review*, 40, 717.

Galanter, Marc and Mia Cahill (1994), '"Most Cases Settle": Judicial Promotion and Regulation of Settlements', *Stanford Law Review*, 46(6), 1339–91.

Gefland, Michele J., Louise Fitzgerald and Fritz Drasgow (1995), 'The Structure of Sexual Harassment: A Confirmatory Analysis Across Cultures and Settings', *Journal of Vocational Behavior*, 47, 164–77.

George, B. Glenn (1993), 'The Back Door: Legitimizing Sexual Harassment Claims', *Boston University Law Review*, 73(1), 1–38.

Gibson, James L. and Gregory A. Calderia (1996), 'The Legal Cultures of Europe', *Law & Society Review*, 30(1), 55–85.

Gilbert, Robert W. (1987), 'Austria's Social Partnership: A Unique Extralegal System of Labour–Management Cooperation', *The Labour Lawyer*, 3, 311–22.

Griffin-Shelley, Eric (1985), 'Sexual Harassment: One Organization's Response', *Journal of Counseling and Development*, 64(1), 72–3.

Gruber, James (1990), 'Methodological Problems and Policy Implications in Sexual Harassment Research', *Population Research and Policy Review*, 9, 235–54.

—— (1997), 'An Epidemiology of Sexual Harassment: Evidence From North America and Europe', in William O'Donohue (ed.), *Sexual Harassment: Theory, Research and Treatment*, Needham Heights, MA: Allyn & Bacon.

—— (1998), 'The Impact of Male Work Environments and Organizational Policies on Women's Experiences of Sexual Harassment', *Gender & Society*, 12(3), 301–20.

Gutek, Barbara A. (1985), *Sex and the Workplace: The Impact of Sexual Behavior and Harassment on Women, Men and Organizations*, San Francisco: CA: Jossey-Bass.

—— (1992), 'Understanding Sexual Harassment at Work', *Notre Dame Journal of Law, Ethics and Public Policy*, 6, 335–58.

Gutek, Barbara A. and Maureen O'Connor (1995), 'The Empirical Basis for the Reasonable Woman Standard', *Journal of Social Issues*, 51(1), 151–66.

Gutek, Barbara A., Bruce Morasch and Aaron Groff Cohen (1983), 'Interpreting Social Sexual Behavior in the Work Setting', *Journal of Vocational Behavior*, 22, 30–48.

Guthrie, Douglas and Louise Marie Roth (1999), 'The State Courts and Maternity Policies in U.S. Organizations: Specifying Institutional Mechanisms', *American Sociological Review*, 64(1), 41–63.

Hamilton, V. Lee and Joseph Sanders (1996), 'Corporate Crime through Citizen's Eyes: Stratification and Responsibility in the United States, Russia and Japan', *Law and Society Review*, 30(3), 513–47.

Haney, Marian C. (1993), 'Litigation of a Sexual Harassment Case after the Civil Rights Act of 1991', *Notre Dame Law Review*, 68, 1037–56.

Hayden, Robert M. (1991), 'The Cultural Logic of a Political Crisis: Common Sense, Hegemony and the Great American Liability Insurance Famine of 1986', *Studies in Law, Politics and Society*, 11, 95–117.

Holzer, Gabriele (1998), 'Haider Business', *Women in Austria*, 6, 141–57.

Hopfgartner, Andrea and Maria Magdalena Zeichen (1988), *Sexuelle Belaestigung am Arbeitsplatz*, Vienna: Bundesministerien fuer Arbeit und Soziales Frauenreferat.

Hunter, Christopher and Kent McClelland (1991), 'Honoring Accounts for Sexual Harassment: A Factorial Survey Analysis', *Sex Roles*, 24(11/12), 725–52.

Husbands, Robert (1992), 'Sexual Harassment Law in Employment: An International Perspective', *International Labour Review*, 131(6), 535–58.

Jensen, Inger W. and Barbara Gutek (1982), 'Attributions and Assignment of Responsibility in Sexual Harassment', *Journal of Social Issues*, 38(4), 121–36.

Judt, Tony (1998), 'Austria and the Ghost of the New Europe', *Women in Austria*, 6, 126–40.

Juliano, Ann and Steward Schwab (1999), 'An Empirical Study of Sexual Harassment Litigation', paper presented at New York University Law School, 20 January 1999; revised, January 2000, as 'Examining the Sweep of Sexual Harassment Cases'.

Kahn, Paul (1999), *The Cultural Study of Law*, Chicago: University of Chicago Press.

Kandel, William L. (1992), 'Mixed Motives, Sexual Harassment and the Civil Rights Act of 1991', *Employee Relations Law Journal*, 17(4), 635–44.
Karrer, H. (1996), 'Tatort-Arbeitsplatz: Sexuälle Belastingung von Frauen, die in Ausbilding stehen', Diplom Arbeit, Institut für Erziehungswissenschaft, Universität.
Kenig, Sylvia and John Ryan (1986), 'Sex Differences in Levels of Tolerance and Attribution of Blame for Sexual Harassment on a University Campus', *Sex Roles*, 15(5/6), 535–49.
Kennedy, David and Keopold Specht (1990), 'Austrian Membership in the European Communities', *Harvard International Law Journal*, 31 (Spring), 407–61.
Konrad, Alison M. and Barbara A. Gutek (1986), 'Impact of Work Experiences on Attitudes Towards Sexual Harassment', *Administrative Science Quarterly*, 31, 422–38.
Korn, Jane Byeff (1993), 'The Fungible Woman and Other Myths of Sexual Harassment', *Tulane Law Review*, 67, 1363–419.
Lach, Denise H. and Patricia A. Gwartney-Gibbs (1993), 'Sociological Perspectives on Sexual Harassment and Workplace Dispute Resolution', *Journal of Vocational Behavior*, 42, 102–15.
Lengnick-Hall, Mark L. (1995), 'Sexual Harassment Research: A Methodological Critique', *Personnel Psychology*, 48, 841–61.
Lester, Toni P. (1995), 'Should Courts Penalize Harassment Victims Who Adopt Passive Coping Strategies?', *Labor Law Journal*, 46 (June), 323–38.
Lipper, Nicolle R. (1992), 'Sexual Harassment in the Workplace: A Comparative Study of Great Britain and the United States', *Comparative Labor Law Journal*, 13, 293–342.
MacKinnon, Catharine (1978), *Sexual Harassment of Working Women*, New Haven, CT: Yale University Press.
Mahoney, Martha R. (1992), 'Exit: Power and the Idea of Leaving in Love, Work and the Confirmation Hearings', *Southern California Law Review*, 65, 1283–319.
Malovich, Deborah and Andrea Stake (1990), 'Sexual Harassment on Campus', *Psychology of Women Quarterly*, 14, 63–81.
McCann, Michael (1992), 'Reform Litigation on Trial', *Law & Social Inquiry*, 17, 715–43.
McCann, Michael and William Haltom (1999), 'Media Framing of Products Liability Lawsuits and the Social Production of Legal Knowledge', Project Description for National Science Foundation proposal.
McCrudden, Christopher (1993), 'The Effectiveness of European Equality Law: National Mechanisms for Enforcing Equality Law in the Light of European Requirements', *Oxford Journal of Legal Studies*, 13(3), 320–67.
Mensch, Elizabeth (1998), 'The History of Mainstream Legal Thought', in

David Kairys (ed.), *The Politics of Law: A Progressive Critique*, New York: Basic Books.

Merry, Sally Engle (1990), *Getting Justice and Getting Even: Legal Consciousness Among Working-Class Americans*, Chicago: University of Chicago Press.

Murrell, Audrey J., Josephine E. Olson and Irene Hanson Frieze (1995), 'Sexual Harassment and Gender Discrimination: A Longitudinal Study of Women Managers', *Journal of Social Issues*, 51(1), 139–49.

Peterka, Josef (1987), 'Equality of Treatment of Men and Women in the Pension Insurance Scheme in Austria', International Social Security Association Studies and Research No. 27, 'Equal Treatment in Social Security'.

Powell, Gary N. (1983), 'Sexual Harassment: Confronting the Issue of Definition', *Business Horizons*, 26(4), 24–8.

Powell, Walter W. and Paul J. DiMaggio (eds) (1991), *The New Institutionalism in Organizational Analysis*, Chicago: University of Chicago Press.

Prager, Tessa, Petra Pichler and Anita Staudacher (1996), 'Die Grapscher Sind Ueberall: Wie Frauen sich gegen sexuelle Belaestiger wehren- und welches Risiko sie dabei tragen', *News*, 19 (9 Mai), 28–32.

Pryor, John B. and Jeanne Day (1988), 'Interpretations of Sexual Harassment: An Attributional Analysis', *Sex Roles*, 18(7/8), 405–17.

Reilly, Timothy, Sandra Carpenter, Valerie Dull and Kim Bartless (1982), 'The Factorial Survey: An Approach to Defining Sexual Harassment on Campus', *Journal of Social Issues*, 38(4), 99–110.

Rickett, Richard (1966), 'A Brief Survey of Austrian History', Vienna: Prachner.

Rosenberger, Sieglinde Katharina (1998), 'Politics, Gender and Equality', in Guenter Beschof, Anton Pelinka and Erika Thurner (eds), *Women in Austria*, New Brunswick, NJ: Transaction Publishers.

Runkel, Philip S. (1994), 'Note. "The Civil Rights Act of 1991: A Continuation of the *Wards Cove* Standard of Business Necessity?"', *William and Mary Law Review*, 35, 1177–239.

Saguy, Abigail C. (1998), 'Discrimination or Abuse of Authority: Making Sexual Harassment Law in France and the United States', paper presented at the 'JOIE' workshop, Princeton University, 12 October.

—— (1999), 'French and U.S. Lawyers Define Sexual Harassment', in Catharine MacKinnon and Reva Siegel (eds), *Symposium on Sexual Harassment*, New Haven, CT: Yale University Press.

—— (2000), 'Sexual Harassment in the United States and France', dissertation, Department of Sociology, Princeton University.

Sanders, Joseph and V. Lee Hamilton (1992), 'Legal Cultures and Punishment Repertoires in Japan, Russia, and the United States', *Law & Society Review*, 26(1), 117–38.

Saperstein, Aron, Bobbi Triolo and Thomas E. Heinzen (1991), 'Ideology or Experience: A Study of Sexual Harassment', *Sex Roles*, 32(11/12), 835–42.

Sanger, Carol (1992), 'The Reasonable Woman and the Ordinary Man', *Southern California Law Review*, 65, 1411–17.

Sarat, Austin (1990), '"The Law Is All Over": Power, Resistance and the Legal Consciousness of the Welfare Poor', *Yale Journal of Law & the Humanities*, 2, 343–79.

Schally, Hugo (1991), 'Austria and the Central European Countries', *Whittier Law Review*, 12, 267–71.

Schneider, Beth E. (1982), 'Consciousness About Sexual Harassment Among Heterosexual and Lesbian Women Workers', *Journal of Social Issues*, 38(4), 75–98.

Schultz, Vicki (1990), 'Telling Stories About Women and Work: Judicial Interpretations of Sex Segregation in the Workplace in Title VII Cases Raising the Lack of Interest Argument', *Harvard Law Review*, 103(8), 1749–843.

Schultz, Vicki (1998), 'Reconceptualizing Sexual Harassment', *Yale Law Journal*, 107, 1683–805.

Selmi, Michael (1996), 'The Value of the EEOC: Reexamining the Agency's Role in Employment Discrimination Law', *Ohio State Law Journal*, 57, 1–64.

Stockdale, Margaret S. (1996), *Sexual Harassment in the Workplace: Perspectives, Frontiers and Response Strategies*, Thousand Oaks, CA: Sage.

Suchman, Mark C. and Mia Cahill (1996), 'The Hired-Gun as Facilitator: The Case of Lawyers in Silicon Valley', *Law and Social Inquiry*, 21, 679–712.

Suchman, Mark C. and Lauren B. Edelman (1996), 'Legal Rational Myths: The New Institutionalism and the Law and Society Tradition', *Law and Social Inquiry*, 21, 903–41.

Summers, Russel J. (1991), 'Determinants of Judgments of and Responses to a Complaint of Sexual Harassment', *Sex Roles*, 25(7/8), 379–92.

Sutton, John and Frank Dobbin (1996), 'Responses to Legal Uncertainty in U.S. Firms, 1955 to 1985', *Amerian Sociological Review*, 61(5), 794–811.

Sutton, John, Frank Dobbin, John Meyer and W. Richard Scott (1994), 'The Legalization of the Workplace', *American Journal of Sociology*, 99(4), 944–71.

Tangri, Sandra S., Marth R. Burt and Leanor B. Johnson (1982), 'Sexual Harassment at Work: Three Explanatory Models', *Journal of Social Issues*, 38(4), 33–54.

Tata, Jasmine (1993), 'The Structure and Phenomenon of Sexual Harassment: Impact of Category of Sexually Harassing Behavior, Gender and Hierarchical Level', *Journal of Applied Social Psychology*, 23(3), 199–211.

Terpstra, David E. and Douglas D. Baker (1986), 'Psychological and

Demographic Correlates of Perception of Sexual Harassment', *Genetic, Social and General Psychology Monographs*, 112(4), 459–78.

Terpstra, David E. and Douglas D. Baker (1988), 'Outcomes of Sexual Harassment Charges', *Academy of Management Journal*, 31(1), 185–94.

Terpstra, David and Douglas Baker (1992), 'Outcomes of Federal Court Decisions on Sexual Harassment', *Academy of Management Journal*, 35, 190–91.

Tinhofer, Andreas (1994), 'Sexuelle Belästigung durch den Geschaeftsfüehrer einer GmbH-sugleich eine Besprechung von ASG Wien 25.2.1994, 25 Cga 461/93', in *Österreichisches Recht der Wirtschaft*, Vienna: Oliver Herzog.

Trubeck, David M. and Marc Galanter (1974), 'Scholars in Self Estrangement: Some Reflections on the Crisis in Law and Development Studies in the United States', *Wisconsin Law Review*, 1974, 1062–102.

Tushnet, Mark (1984), 'Critical Legal Studies and Constitutional Law: An Essay in Deconstruction', *Stanford Law Review*, 36, 623–47.

United States Merit Systems Protection Board (1981), *Sexual Harassment in the Federal Workplace: Is It A Problem?*, Washington, DC: Office of Merit Systems Review and Studies/Government Printing Office.

United States Merit Systems Protection Board (1988), *Sexual Harassment in the Federal Workplace: An Update*, Washington DC: Office of Merit Systems and Review Studies/Government Printing Office.

Valiente, Celia (1998), 'Sexual Harassment in the Workplace: Equality Policies in Post-Authoritarian Spain', pp. 169–79 in Terrell Carver and Veronique Mottier (eds), *Politics of Sexuality: Identity, Gender, Citizenship*, London and New York: Routledge.

Valiente, Celia (2000), 'Left or Right: Does It Make Any Difference? Central-State Sexual Harassment Policies in Spain', paper presented at the Twelfth International Conference of Europeanists, Chicago, 30 March–1 April.

Webb, Susan L. (1994), *Shock Waves: The Global Impact of Sexual Harassment*, New York: MasterMedia Limited.

Weeks, Elaine Lunsford, Jacqueline M. Boles, Albeno P. Garbin and John Blount (1986), 'The Transformation of Sexual Harassment from a Private Trouble into a Public Issue', *Sociological Inquiry*, 56, 432–55.

Weick, Karl E. (1995), *Sensemaking in Organizations*, Thousand Oaks, CA: Sage.

Weiss, Marley (1993), 'The Impact of the European Community on Labor Law: Some American Comparisons', *Chicago-Kent Law Review*, 68(3), 1427–67.

Wilhelm, Georg (1993), 'Gleichbehandlung Der Geschlecter', *Ecolex*, February.

Zippel, Kathrina (1999), 'Austria', in Directorate-General for Employment European Commission, Industrial Relations and Social Affairs (ed.), *Sexual*

Harassment at the Workplace in the European Union, 47–55, Luxembourg: Office for Official Publications of the European Communities.

Zippel, Kathrina (2000), *Policies Against Sexual Harassment: Gender Equality Policies in Germany, the European Union and the United States in Comparative Perspective*, Dissertation, Department of Sociology, University of Wisconsin-Madison.

Index